"Most people make life's important decisions by using their intellect. They think and become logical. Thus their path in life becomes *path-o-logical*.

As a physician, I know how important our feelings are. We store a lifetime of feelings in our bodies. If not felt and responded to, they lead to disease—once again, a state of pathology.

Learn to focus, and let the wisdom of your body teach you what it feels like to be happy. The wisdom of this book can help you heal the pathology.

This book is an excellent resource for healing your life and body while guiding you to your life's true path."

> —Bernie Siegel, M.D., author of *Love, Medicine, and Miracles; Peace, Love, and Healing;* and *How to Live Between Office Visits*

"I have included Ann Weiser Cornell's Focusing work in Intuitive Training classes with excellent results. I see the Focusing technique as an invaluable tool for students of the inner life, particularly psychic-intuitive training."

> —Helen Palmer, author of *The Enneagram*

THE POWER OF FOCUSING

Ann Weiser Cornell, Ph.D.

MJF BOOKS
NEW YORK

Published by MJF Books
Fine Communications
322 Eighth Avenue
New York, NY 10001

The Power of Focusing
LC Control Number 98-67591
ISBN-13: 978-1-56731-297-3
ISBN-10: 1-56731-297-7

This edition published by arrangement with New Harbinger Publications, Inc.

Text Design by Tracy Marie Powell

Printed in the United States of America.

MJF Books and the MJF colophon are trademarks of Fine Creative Media, Inc.

QM   15   14   13   12   11   10

for Bryan,
who does want to know

Contents

Preface

I first encountered Focusing in 1972, when I was a graduate student in linguistics at the University of Chicago. A sudden and painful breakup with a boyfriend a few months before had made me realize that there was a great deal going on inside of me beneath my conscious awareness, and I resolved to find a way to get to know that deeper me.

Friends told me that a man named Gene Gendlin was teaching something called Focusing on Sunday nights in a community center. I went to one of the meetings, and I was both fascinated and frustrated. Fascinated because I knew this was just what I was looking for: a simple and powerful way to get to know what I really felt and wanted. Frustrated because it was hard for me to learn. I didn't understand what I was being asked to do, and when I tried to do what I thought they were teaching, nothing happened.

Eventually, with the help of patient friends, I did learn Focusing, and it became my companion through many life changes. In 1980, after I left linguistics teaching and was searching for another career, Gene Gendlin invited me to teach Focusing with him. In 1983, after assisting Gene in many workshops in Chicago, I moved to California and began teaching Focusing on my own.

I never forgot the difficulties I had had learning Focusing, and I resolved to find ways to improve the teaching of Focusing so anyone could learn it. My background in linguistics made me especially sensitive to language, and I realized that the precise language used in Focusing teaching can help or hinder the process enormously. I wrote two manuals, one for Focusing students and one for Focusing guides, so that other teachers could make use of these insights as well.

At the end of 1994 two things happened. First, I made another breakthrough in teaching, with the inspiration of Carol Bellin and Carol LaDue, and found a way of presenting Focusing that was even more successful. Second, New Harbinger asked me to write this book. The first half of 1995 was a richly creative time, as I tested the new language of teaching I had discovered during workshops in California, Australia, and Maryland—and wrote. The teaching flowed, and so did the writing. This book now stands as my new Focusing manual, built on the experience of teaching hundreds of Focusing workshops over fifteen years.

I love Focusing. It is a beautiful, subtle, rich, empowering process which is now woven into the fabric of my life. I can hardly say that I *do* Focusing; it is more that I *live* Focusing. The gifts that it has brought me include a spiritual opening that I never expected.

I'm convinced that the times we live in require each of us to be fully and courageously who we are. Focusing is the fastest way I know to get to the truth of ourselves and to live it. Teaching Focusing is more than a profession for me; it is a passion. If I can help you further in your journey with Focusing, please write to me; my address and phone and fax numbers are at the back of this book.

No book is the work of only one person. I'd especially like to thank Barbara McGavin, who spent days reading and responding to early drafts; many of her words found their way into the final book. Barbara's brilliance and her dedication to excellent Focusing teaching are gifts to us all.

I'd like to thank Gene Gendlin, my teacher, without whom we would not have been able to see and understand what Focusing is, much less how to teach it.

I'd like to thank Neil Friedman, a therapist who has written much about Focusing, and who in his own way was the angel who made this book possible.

I'd like to appreciate my other colleagues and teachers who were part of the development of Focusing to the point where it could be written about this way: Carol Bellin, Reva Bernstein, Les Brunswick, Lakme Elior, Elfie Hinterkopf, Bebe Simon, and many more.

For reading drafts of this book and making useful suggestions, I'd like to thank: Helene G. Brenner, Marilyn Skelton Jellison, Larry Letich, Judy Levy, Judith Ann Perlin, Roger Pritchard, Bebe Simon, Martha Sloss, and John Swinburne.

I'd like to thank the dear friends who let me write in their homes and be part of their families while I was traveling, especially Sebastiaan and Kate, and Larry and Helene.

More than I can say, I appreciate all my students who let me test this material on them and who taught me so much.

And a special thanks to the fine people at New Harbinger who are too good to be mere publishers; they must be angels in disguise.

Chapter One

What Is Focusing?

Whenever Jenny needed to speak up about herself, she got a choking sensation in her throat. The more important the situation was to her, the stronger she felt the choking. Job interviews and class presentations were painful, nearly impossible. She had been to many therapists and tried many techniques to try to get rid of this choking sensation, without results. She diagnosed herself as "self-defeating, masochistic, always sabotaging myself."

Then Jenny heard about Focusing. She heard that Focusing is a way of listening to your body with compassion, without assumptions. She heard that many people experience profound and lasting change from this kind of inner listening. She was doubtful. It sounded too simple! But she was willing to give it a try, because she was desperate for something to work.

One thing that intrigued Jenny was that Focusing is a skill, not a therapeutic technique. Although many therapists incorporate Focusing in their work, Jenny would be able to learn Focusing without going to a therapist. She liked the idea of learning a skill that she would be able to use, not only for the choking sensation but for any issue in her life, on her own, without needing to pay someone.

When Jenny came in for her Focusing lesson and told me her situation, I had a strong feeling that Focusing could help her. I've taught Focusing to many hundreds of people over the years, and Jenny's circumstance was classic. Her body was already speaking to her. She just needed to learn how to hear its message.

I asked Jenny if she was feeling the choking at that very moment.

"Yes. I can feel it. It's here now because I'm learning a new technique with you, and I feel I have to do well."

I asked her to describe what it felt like. She looked a little surprised, and said, "Choking, of course!" I asked her to go back to the sensation and check the word "choking" to make sure that word was the right word for how it felt.

She looked thoughtful. "Actually," she said slowly, "it's more like a hand squeezing."

Now Jenny's eyes were closed and she was concentrating inwardly. I asked her to gently say hello to the hand squeezing sensation. "Just say to it, 'Yes, I know you're there.' "

This was a completely new attitude for her. "I've never sort of looked it in the eye before; I've just tried to get rid of it." So this new attitude took a while to find, but when she did, there was a definite sense of bodily relief: "It's still there, but it's not painful anymore. It's almost like, now that it has my attention, it doesn't need to hurt me."

Then I asked Jenny to imagine that she was sitting down with the sensation as she would sit with a friend, compassionate and curious about how the friend was feeling.

Jenny was silent for several minutes, eyes closed, sensing. Then her eyes opened in astonishment. "Wow. I *never* dreamed it would say something like that. That's really amazing."

I waited, knowing that she would tell me the rest in her own time.

In a moment she spoke again. "It says . . . it says it cares about me! It says it's just trying to keep me from making mistakes!"

"And how does it feel now?" I asked.

"The choking or squeezing is completely gone. My throat feels open and relaxed. There's a good warm feeling spreading all through my body. This is really amazing. I never thought it would change like this!"

What is Focusing?

Focusing is a body-oriented process of self-awareness and emotional healing. It's as simple as noticing how you feel—and then having a conversation with your feelings in which *you* do most of the listening. Focusing starts with the familiar experience of feeling something in your body that is about what is going on in your life. When you feel jittery in your stomach as you stand up to speak, or when you feel tightness in your chest as you anticipate making a crucial phone call, you are experiencing what we call a "felt sense"—a body sensation that is meaningful.

So what do you do when you have a jittery feeling or a tightness or a choking sensation in your throat? If you're like most of us, you try to get rid of it. Maybe you curse it a little: "Why does this stupid feeling have to come now, just when I need to be my best?" Or maybe you put yourself down: "If I were a better person, I wouldn't freeze up this way." Maybe you do deep breathing exercises, or have a drink or a cigarette.

What doesn't occur to you, unless you know Focusing, is to listen to the feeling, to let *it* speak to *you*.

And yet, when you let the feeling speak to you, you are allowing yourself to be open to the depth and richness of your whole self. Furthermore, when you listen to the feeling, it is much more likely to relax, release, and let you go on with what you're doing in a clear and centered way. You might even move forward in this area of your life in ways that surprise and delight you.

Focusing is the process of listening to your body in a gentle, accepting way and hearing the messages that your inner self is sending you. It's a process of honoring the wisdom that you have inside you, becoming aware of the subtle level of knowing that speaks to you through your body.

The results of listening to your body are insight, physical release, and positive life change. You understand yourself better, you feel better, *and* you act in ways that are more likely to create the life you want.

The discovery of Focusing

In the early 1960s, Professor Eugene Gendlin at the University of Chicago began research into the question: "Why is psychotherapy helpful for some people, but not others?" He and his colleagues studied tapes of hundreds of therapy sessions. They taped the entire course of therapy, from the first session to the last, with many different therapists and clients. Then they asked both the therapists and the clients to rate whether the therapy had been successful, and they also used psychological tests to determine if there had been positive change. If all three agreed—therapist, client, and independent test—then that course of therapy was used in the study. The result was two groups of tapes: successful versus unsuccessful psychotherapy.

The researchers then compared the tapes to see if they could determine what made the difference between success and failure. They first listened to the therapists on the tapes. Common sense suggested that there would be something about the therapist's behavior that would determine whether therapy was successful or not. Surely the therapists in the successful therapy were somehow more empathic, or more genuine, or more accepting, or more brilliant. . . . But in fact there was *no significant difference* in therapist behavior. In both sets of tapes, the therapists were essentially the same. The therapists were doing their best—and some clients were getting better, while others were not.

Then the researchers listened to the clients on the tapes, and that is when they made a fascinating and important discovery: there *was* a difference between the successful therapy clients and the unsuccessful ones. And it was a difference that could be heard in the first or second session—in the *clients*. Whatever this was, it wasn't something that the successful clients learned how to do because of the therapy; it was something they were already doing, able to do, when they walked in the door.

Gendlin and the other researchers found, to their surprise, that they could predict success in therapy by listening to the tapes of anyone's first two therapy sessions. Listening to the client, they could actually tell whether or not the therapy would be ultimately successful!

So what was this? What was it that the researchers could hear on the tapes, that allowed them to predict whether the therapy would be successful?

What they heard was this: at some point in the session, the successful therapy clients would *slow down* their talk, become *less articulate*, and begin to *grope for words* to describe something that they were feeling at that moment. If you listened to the tapes, you would hear something like this: "Hmmm. How would I describe this? It's right *here*. It's . . . uh . . . it's . . . it's not exactly anger . . . hmmm." Often the clients would mention that they experienced this feeling in their bodies, saying things like, "It's right here in my chest," or "I have this funny feeling in my stomach."

So the successful therapy clients had a vague, hard-to-describe body awareness that they were directly sensing during the session. By contrast, the unsuccessful therapy clients stayed articulate through the whole session! They stayed "up in their heads." They didn't sense in their bodies, and they never directly felt something that at first was hard to describe. No matter how much they analyzed their problems, or explained them, or thought about them, or cried about them, their therapy was ultimately unsuccessful.

Eugene Gendlin determined to find out how to teach the skill that made all the difference between successful and unsuccessful therapy. As a therapist himself, he didn't want to merely sit back and watch as some of his clients got better and others did not. He wanted to help everyone.

Gendlin did find a way to teach this powerful and effective skill of emotional healing, and he called it "Focusing." At first he thought Focusing would only be useful to improve psychotherapy. But then people started asking him to teach them Focusing for other purposes: as a self-help skill to use instead of therapy, to make decisions, to help with creative projects. In 1978 he published a book called *Focusing* which sold hundreds of thousands of copies. The interest in Focusing was so great that Gendlin started offering workshops and started the Focusing Institute to support the growing worldwide network of people using Focusing. (See the "Resources" section at the back of this book for more information about how you can connect with this network.)

Focusing is a natural skill that was discovered, not invented. It was discovered by looking at what people are doing when they are changing successfully. Focusing ability is the birthright of every person: we were all born with the ability to know how we feel from moment to moment. But for most of us, the experiences of hurt and alienation in our childhood and from our culture have caused us to lose trust in our bodies and our feelings. We need to re-learn Focusing.

Who benefits from Focusing?

Focusing is a very broad-purpose skill. It isn't intended for one single purpose, but for many. The wonderful thing is that you can learn

Focusing and then use it whenever you need it for the rest of your life. Jenny's story, told at the beginning of the book, is an example of how to use Focusing to understand and change an intrusive body signal, such as a choking sensation. Here are some of the other ways you might benefit from Focusing.

If you feel stuck in your therapy

Often people who are in psychotherapy but feel stuck decide to learn Focusing in order to get their therapy moving again. They feel their therapy progressed for a while, but then bogged down somehow. "I keep saying the same things, getting the same insights," one woman reported. "I know there's something I'm not getting to, but I don't know what."

Some therapists incorporate Focusing techniques in their therapy. Others recommend their clients learn Focusing and practice it between sessions. If you're in therapy now and you would like your therapist to use Focusing, see Chapter Eleven, "If You're in Therapy."

If you'd like to know better what you feel and want

Many people are not in touch with their feelings and their wants. Often men are trained to ignore and set aside feelings, especially "weaker" and more tender feelings like fear and sadness. "People ask me how I feel and I draw a blank. It's like there's nothing there." Often women are trained to defer to others, to set their own feelings aside and put others' feelings first. As a consequence, we don't even know what we feel and want. We're cut off from our bodies, from the source of knowing how we feel. Focusing brings us back into our bodies and back into contact with what is real for us, our feelings, wants, and needs.

If you'd like a way to handle overwhelming emotions

Strong feelings like sadness, fear, or anger can sometimes feel overwhelming. They can wash over us like ocean waves, shake us like a windstorm, and we can feel helpless next to their power. But these emotions are strong for a reason. They have an important story to tell;

they are bringing back an important piece of our wholeness. Focusing lets you hear the story and receive the gifts from these strong emotions without getting overwhelmed. With Focusing you learn how to have a comfortable relationship with strong feelings, how to acknowledge them and listen to them, instead of being drowned by them.

If you'd like to release action blocks or addictions

An action block is any place in your life where you want to do something but you don't. The most common action blocks are organization blocks (like never getting your desk organized) and writer's block. Procrastination is the all-purpose block. If you can fill in the blank in this sentence: "I want to _____ , but I don't," then you have an action block.

Addictions work like action blocks in reverse. With an addiction, the sentence is, "I want to stop _____ , but I don't."

Focusing helps you release action blocks or addictions by enabling you to listen compassionately to the part of you that is responsible for the block or addiction, and gain its cooperation.

If you'd like to release self-criticism and increase self-love and acceptance

"You've failed again. You'll always fail. You might as well give up now."

"There's something profoundly wrong with you. You're flawed in a way that can never be fixed."

"You're weird. You'd better not let anyone see how weird you are—they won't want to be friends with you."

Who is saying these terrible things to you? If you're like most of us, you say them to yourself. We are typically more harsh and cruel to ourselves than we are to anyone else. Focusing has powerful tools for releasing you from self-criticism and other forms of inner sabotage. You'll learn to turn your inner Critic into an ally and supporter, and you'll grow in love and acceptance for all parts of yourself. This self-acceptance in turn allows deeper and faster change in the areas of your life that need to change.

If you'd like to make clear and centered decisions

Everyone needs to make decisions, every day. Some are small, such as "What shall I have for dinner?" Some are large, such as "What will I do with the rest of my life?" If decision making isn't easy for you, every day can be a minefield. Confusion, self-doubt, and anxiety are a few of the companions of a difficult decision-making process.

"I want to learn Focusing," one man told me, "because I realize that my decision making always falls back on what I *should* do, according to other people, or society. And I don't want that."

The classical way of making a decision is to draw a line down the middle of a sheet of paper and list all the "pros" on one side, all the "cons" on the other. Have you ever done that and found yourself at the end as undecided as ever? The difficulty is that this is a purely logical way of decision making, and logic uses only one part of us. We need to make decisions, especially important ones, from our whole self. Focusing is a great tool for decision making because it helps you sense the rightness of the choice you are making, at a level beyond logical analysis. You will be able to make a choice that is right for you *holistically*, that is, taking in and integrating all factors at once.

The wisdom of the body

It is becoming common knowledge that we can consult our bodies about what is right for us to eat and how much exercise we need. Many people now understand that our bodies "know" what good health is, and that our bodies can show us how to find our way to optimum physical health if we so desire. But to see the scope of the body's wisdom as only physical is to take much too narrow a view. There is much more.

The truth is that our bodies are wise in many ways hardly ever acknowledged by our culture. Our bodies carry knowledge about how we are living our lives, about what we need to be more fully ourselves, about what we value and believe, about what has hurt us emotionally and how to heal it. Our bodies know which people around us are the ones who bring out the best in us, and which people deplete and diminish us. Our bodies know what is the right next step to bring us to more fulfilling and rewarding lives.

Our minds alone do not know these things. Our minds can remember the past, repeat what others have told us, and invent any number of possible futures to be either wishful or anxious about. But the past and the future, the primary domains of the mind, are not the place where change can happen. Change happens in the present. The gift of the body is that it is always in present time, always *here*. To move into the part of you that has the power to transform your life, all you need to do is to bring your awareness to your body.

Focusing is the way in to this vast realm of knowledge and this exciting potential for change. Focusing lets you form a trusting relationship with your body so you can begin to hear the wisdom of this vast part of yourself that is accessible through body awareness. Focusing lets you listen to the whispers of your body before it has to shout. Focusing is the key to changing your life in a way that satisfies your inner sense of rightness.

In the next chapter, we'd like to give you a "tour" of the Focusing process, so you'll get an impression of what it's like to do Focusing. In Chapter Three, we'll set the stage for your own Focusing by showing you how to create an inner climate of safety and trust. In Chapters Four and Five, we'll show you how to do Focusing yourself. In Chapter Six, we show you how to receive the gifts—the positive feelings—that result from Focusing. Chapter Seven contains a number of stories about people using Focusing for particular purposes, such as making decisions, or handling overwhelming feelings. In Chapter Eight, we'll do "troubleshooting," and help you with some of the most typical problems and questions. Chapters Nine, Ten, and Eleven are about Focusing with a friend, with your clients if you're a therapist, and with your therapist if you're a therapy client.

Chapter Two

A Focusing Process

To give you a "tour" of the Focusing process, I'd like to tell you the story of Ted, and how he used Focusing to find out how he felt. I'll point out the various Focusing attitudes and skills that Ted is using at different stages along the way.

Ted was always frustrated when his wife asked him, "How do you feel?" and he had no idea how to answer. His wife was so persistent in wanting to know his feelings that he realized he had never known how to answer that question. He had never understood how people knew how they were feeling.

"She asks me how I feel and I draw a blank," he told me. "It's like there's nothing there."

So Ted decided to learn Focusing. First he learned to be aware of his inner body sensations, especially in his throat, chest, and stomach. This was new for him; he had never been encouraged to notice his body. His father and older brothers had never talked about feelings. In high school and college he had played sports, and it had been better *not* to pay too close attention to the aches and injuries he had.

So when Ted first tried closing his eyes and sensing in his body, it was like going into unfamiliar territory. It took him a while just to get "in there." He reminded himself of the last time he had had a cold and checked his throat as if seeing if it was still sore. No . . . but at least his awareness was in his throat. From there, it was fairly easy to also sense in his chest and in his stomach.

Focusing begins with bringing awareness into the body,
especially the throat, chest, stomach, and abdomen.

At first Ted felt nothing, and he was discouraged and felt like quitting. But then he tried the Focusing question, "What wants my awareness now?" and just waited, noticing anything. He realized that his stomach felt tightly clenched—and that it had probably been feeling that way for a long time. He didn't feel *nothing*, he just felt *normal*—and normal was "clenched."

We don't try to find a feeling, or try to make something happen,
but we invite something to be felt by asking a gentle, open
question such as "What wants my awareness now?"

Ted stayed with the clenched feeling, acknowledging it. He found that when he said hello to it, he felt a slight relief. It was still there, but it didn't feel quite so immovable. He tried naming it, and the word "clenched" fit fairly well, well enough for now.

When we first find a feeling, we acknowledge it by saying an
inner hello to it, and then we describe or name it.

Then Ted settled down to get to know the clenched feeling better. He knew it had been there a long time, and he was genuinely curious and interested in what he might learn. This was the first time he had ever considered that a feeling like this might have a reason to be there, other than just being some flaw in him.

In the next stage of Focusing, we sit down with the feeling to get
to know it better, with an attitude of interested curiosity.

At first the feeling felt like a solid wall, no meaning, a blank. Then he began to get the idea that this clenched part of him was scared. He checked the word "scared" with the feeling and felt a little extra tightening. Yes! "Scared" was right.

We take time to allow a little more meaning to come from the
feeling, perhaps a word for an emotional quality. Then we check
the word with the feeling, to make sure it feels right.

Ted noticed that his first tendency was to tell his stomach that there was no reason to be scared. But he knew that in Focusing you accept that there is *some* good reason for every feeling, even if you don't know what it is yet. So he stayed with the clenched, scared feeling. He just breathed for a while, letting it be. Then he asked it, "Please tell me, what gets you so scared?"

We are not in a hurry. We create an inner atmosphere of no pressure, just being with what's there. We ask gentle questions as a way of inviting the feeling to tell us more.

The answer took a while to feel, but by now Ted was learning patience. He began to get the feeling of what an effort this clenched part of him was making, to stay hard and tough. "It's scared," he realized, "and it's also scared to show that it's scared." As he said this, he felt a relaxing in his stomach, as if something inside him was saying, "I'm glad you heard me."

The relaxing felt good, and Ted was tempted to stop Focusing right there. He certainly could have stopped and come back to his body another time. But he was still curious, and his stomach was still clenched, just not so tightly as before.

In Focusing, change comes in steps, small (usually) realizations, each one of which feels right and makes some difference in the body. After each one, we could stop and focus again another time, or we could keep going, perhaps with another gentle question.

He asked the clenched place the question again, as gently as he might have asked one of his own kids after a nightmare, "So what is it that's so scary for you right now?" He flashed on a memory of his father slumped in an armchair, his mother standing in the doorway with an angry look on her face. The words came: "I can't fail."

"I hear you," Ted whispered to his body. "You feel like it's not OK to fail."

In Ted's stomach there came a deep releasing, like something letting go with relief. Ted had the experience of exploring a new sensation: a completely relaxed stomach for the first time in years! What a gift!

The meaning that is carried in the body is sometimes connected with a memory, a belief or attitude, or an unmet need or an unexpressed part of ourselves. There is no need to "fix" or "solve" the problem. Acknowledging the message, really hearing it, is all that is needed to bring deep relief.

To complete his Focusing session, Ted took some time to enjoy his new, relaxed feeling. He noticed that part of him had a tendency to tighten up again, asking, "But how does this solve the problem?" Gently but firmly he set this question aside and went back to simply sensing his body. He asked if this might be a good place to stop Focusing for now, and he got the distinct feeling of wanting to sense this relaxed feeling quietly for a few more minutes. So he did that. Then he thanked his body, and said he'd be back. Slowly, several minutes after he'd first been ready to stop, he opened his eyes.

> *Ending a Focusing session happens slowly and respectfully. We may want to stay for a while with good feelings. We thank the body, and say we'll be back.*

Later that day, when Ted was on the phone with a client, he noticed his stomach clenching again. After the call ended, he paused a few minutes before his next call, and just stayed with the feeling in his stomach. He realized that when he had heard an angry and impatient tone in the client's voice, it had triggered the place in him that was afraid of failure. When he realized that, the clenching released.

> *Life circumstances may bring back feelings that were there in the Focusing session. This is an opportunity for "mini-Focusing"— a little bit of Focusing in the midst of life.*

That evening when Ted saw his wife, she asked him, "How are you feeling?" Ted replied, "I'm excited and I'm a little scared, because I'm learning something new, and I don't know where it's going to take me." After he said it he checked in his body and it was true, he *was* feeling excited and a little scared. Ted's wife was so surprised she was speechless—all she could do was give him a big hug.

Chapter Three

Focusing in Safety and Trust

Imagine that you are in a meadow, at the edge of a forest. As you stand there quietly, you see a shy animal peeking out of the woods. You know that this animal is not dangerous to you, nor you to it, and you would like to help it feel safe with you. What would you do? What mood would you try to create? What would you *not* do?

You would not run toward it, shouting. You would be still and patient. If you moved, you would move slowly and gently. You would be attentive to it, interested in it, watching it carefully for signs that it might be OK for you to move a little closer.

Focusing is a process of listening to something inside you that wants to communicate with you. And yet, like a shy animal, it may first need to discover that you are trustworthy, and that you have created a safe place for it, before it can deliver its message. In this chapter we will talk about how to create the climate of safety and trust in your inner world that makes Focusing possible.

Letting it be as it is

Take a moment to notice what you are feeling right now and see if it is possible to simply let the feeling be there. Good, bad, or indifferent; angry, sad, or scared; bored, restless, or joyful—just notice how you are right now, and notice if you can say, "Yes, that is how I feel."

Notice whether it is difficult or unfamiliar to let your feelings be there. You may have a tendency, as many people do, to judge your feelings as soon as you notice them: "I shouldn't be feeling that way. What a horrible person I am to feel that!" You may try to be "reasonable" about your feelings: "There's no reason to be scared." Or you may try to talk yourself out of your feelings: "Oh, it's not that bad. Other people have it worse." Or you may try to analyze your feelings, asking yourself: "Why? Why do I always feel this way? Why can't I change?"

As you may have noticed, none of these ways is effective in helping you change. Every time you judge yourself, or try to talk yourself out of your feelings, or try to figure out why you are feeling this way, you just stay in the same place, and probably feel even worse about yourself.

But I can tell you with absolute assurance, for I've seen this hundreds of times and never seen it fail: when you allow your feelings to be as they are, then they *can* change. When you *try* to change them, they stay unchanged. Gene Gendlin put it so well:

> *What is split off, not felt, remains the same. When it is felt, it changes. Most people don't know this. They think that by not permitting the feeling of their negative ways they make themselves good. On the contrary, that keeps these negatives static, the same from year to year. A few moments of feeling it in your body allows it to change. If there is in you something bad or sick or unsound, let it inwardly be, and breathe. That's the only way it can evolve and change into the form it needs.*

The inner climate of *letting it inwardly be* is necessary for inner change. And this is the good news. You may think that allowing your feelings to be will make them bigger, or will give them permission to go out of control. You will find that just the opposite is the case. Your feelings get bigger and more painful when they *aren't* allowed to be. When they *are* allowed to be, they settle down to have a conversation with you, and that conversation leads to change, as we will see.

Being in a relationship with your feelings

Being in a relationship with your inner experience allows you to be *with* your feelings, not *in* them. Many people think that the only way to change strong emotions is to jump right into the middle of them, feel them intensely, and get *through* them. When you're reluctant to do that, you may call yourself "resistant" and "afraid to change."

Focusing, however, teaches us that change comes more easily from a *relationship* with your feelings. And you can't have a relationship with something if you're up to your neck in it!

Think of your emotions as a big lake. You have a choice: you can plunge into the lake, or you can sit next to it. Focusing works best when you "sit next to" what you feel instead of plunging into it.

When you have a relationship with something, you can sense it as a whole. When you're in the middle of it, it's harder to know it—just as it's hard for a fish to know water. When I assisted Gene Gendlin in teaching Focusing he would say, "If you want to know what the soup smells like, it's better not to stick your head in it."

When you have a relationship with what's there, you are able to be its listener. It is able to tell you its story. If you *are* it, then there's no one else to hear the story. This inner relationship is how you give yourself the healing presence that is so powerful and helpful.

If you find yourself saying, "I am sad," try changing that to "*Part of me* is sad," or "I *have* a sad feeling," or "*I'm aware of something* that feels sad." Now the sad feeling becomes something you can *be with* instead of feeling all over, because it's part of you, not all of you.

Being a good listener to your self

Do you remember a time when someone listened to you, really listened? Do you remember how good it felt to be heard? Perhaps you began to understand yourself better, and you clarified what you were thinking and feeling, simply because someone was listening.

Perhaps you also remember a time when you wanted to express yourself and be heard, but the other person didn't hear you. Instead, perhaps they criticized, or told you about their own experience, or offered well-meaning advice. Advice isn't listening. If you wanted to be heard and you got criticism or advice instead, you probably became more confused or frustrated or upset instead of more clear. And you probably felt you wouldn't come back to that person again when you needed to be heard.

Focusing is being a good listener to your inner self. There are parts of you that want to be heard, without judgment, without criticism, without advice. In Focusing, you can give yourself that non-judgmental listening that feels good and brings greater clarity.

The qualities of good listening are:

- A welcoming presence
- Holding the space
- Hearing the essence
- Staying in present time.

A welcoming presence means you are interested in everything you become aware of inside. Each feeling you become aware of, no matter how ugly or negative it appears at first, has a good reason for being the way it is. A welcoming presence gives it the space to be and breathe, evolve and transform.

Holding the space means bringing your awareness to your inner world and holding it there. It's as if you're saying to your inner self, "I'm here and I'm staying with you."

Hearing the essence means listening for what is longing to be heard. When something first comes forward, its message may be difficult to understand. If you keep listening for what "it" wants you to hear, the message will become clearer and clearer.

Staying in present time means not being distracted by dwelling on what happened in the past, or on fantasies or fears about the future. It means staying in touch with how you're feeling in your body right now, even when what you are focusing on is related to the past or the future. Whenever you find you have drifted away from the present, ask yourself, "How am I feeling in my body right now? What am I aware of right now?"

Being a friend to your felt sense

Focusing is like being a friend to your own inner experience. The qualities of true friendship include acknowledging, allowing, patience, curiosity, respect, warmth, welcome, empathy, compassion, and love. If you don't feel you can be *that* much of a friend to yourself immediately, don't worry—you'll be able to build up to it, step by step. And the first step is as simple as saying hello.

When you notice you're having a feeling, say to the feeling, "Hello. I know you're there." This might seem ridiculously simple, but it's actually such a powerfully helpful move that you'll probably feel relief just from doing this alone. It's amazing how often we don't do this. We ignore how we feel, we try to get rid of how we feel, we argue with how we feel—but we're not actually acknowledging how we feel. We treat our felt senses like unwelcome party guests, to be talked *about* but never directly spoken *to*.

If your felt senses are at all scary or intense, saying hello becomes even more important. "I feel this constriction in my chest, and it's getting tighter and tighter!" said Rebecca. "You might just say hello to it," I suggested. "Oh! Now it's easing up quite a bit!" she reported, amazed that simply acknowledging could make such a difference.

The reason that acknowledging is so powerful is that your felt senses are here to communicate with you. Excuse me for talking about felt senses as if they were people, but the truth is, they *want* you to listen. They want to be heard. That constriction was probably getting tighter and tighter because it was panicked about whether it would be heard. As soon as Rebecca acknowledged it, it was able to relax a little, because it knew that she knew it was there, and that she would listen to its story.

I cannot emphasize enough how important it is to say hello to what you find in your body. I've seen over and over how people skip over this step and find themselves in trouble. For example, Catherine had a tightness in her shoulders that she had been feeling for weeks. She wanted to focus on it. The people in the workshop watched as she rolled her neck impatiently and said, "I want to ask this what it's all about, but it won't talk to me. I feel stuck." Then she looked down at the card she had received at the beginning of the workshop and saw the sentence, *I'm saying hello to what's here*. "Oh," she said, "I haven't said hello to it yet."

Then the other workshop participants saw a remarkable transformation. Catherine's face flushed, her head stopped rolling, and tears sprang to her eyes. "I've *never* said hello to it!" she exclaimed. "I've called it bad, I've tried to get rid of it, I've shamed it, I've tried to fix it—but I've never actually said hello." From that moment on the tightness in her shoulders began to release and by the end of the session, after it had given its message, Catherine experienced her body quite differently.

Focusing is about having a positive and supportive *relationship* with yourself. Every relationship begins with hello. It isn't respectful to start a conversation without first saying hello. So give your felt sense a hello first of all, and the rest of your friendship with it will naturally follow.

When you're not feeling friendly

Sometimes you just can't bring yourself to be friendly to your felt sense. And that's OK—you can still do Focusing. Just move your awareness to the part of you that isn't feeling friendly. Say hello to *that*. The not-friendly feeling, whatever it is, becomes the new felt sense.

Tom was feeling fear in his belly. He recognized it as an old fear, one that he had felt many times before. When he asked himself to be "like a friend" to this fear, he could feel an angry impatience rising in his body. "I'm so sick of always getting scared, right when things are getting good!"

So Tom said hello to the angry, impatient feeling. This is different from staying *in* the anger and impatience, continuing to *be* angry and impatient. This is more like stepping aside slightly, noticing or "witnessing" what is felt. Instead of trying to force himself to be friendly to the original feeling, the fear, Tom simply moved his friendly attitude to the anger and impatience about the fear.

When something is in the way of being friendly and accepting, we call this the *feeling about the feeling*. It might be: "I'm angry about this fear," or "I'm afraid of this sadness," or "I'm impatient with this stuck place."

Trying to push your way past this feeling won't work. If you ignore it, your Focusing will get stuck at this exact point. That's because the feeling about the feeling is a signal that something else is coming up that needs attention.

Two things may happen, and they're both fine. Often, after you've spent some time with the feeling about the feeling, it relaxes and lets you go back to the original feeling. But sometimes the whole remainder of the session is about the feeling about the feeling. This is wonderfully rewarding, because it often relates to a central part of how you are in the world. When it changes, ripples of change spread through your whole life.

Hearing all the voices

We often believe that we must feel only one way about something. Ambivalence is wrong, we think. But it is the most natural thing in the world to have mixed feelings. A part of us wants to get to know someone better, another part of us is scared to get too close. A part of us feels angry that we haven't been consulted in a decision, but another part is frightened of the consequences of expressing that anger.

Focusing allows all the parts of our self to be heard. And when their messages have been received, they change. You don't have to choose between different parts; they can all be there at the same time. They can each have their own space. And a special kind of magic can happen when we are able to be with all the different parts. Out of that can come something that is better than and different from any of the parts, and yet all the parts have given something essential to the new synthesis.

We are complex beings in an ambiguous world. We are full of often contradictory feelings and thoughts. It can be liberating to realize that we don't have to be monolithic. With Focusing, we learn how to welcome, acknowledge, and accept all our responses to life—whatever they are. We can feel all our variety and subtlety, all our richness and complexity.

The wisdom of not knowing

Be willing to approach your inner experience without thinking that you know all about it already. This is the attitude of *not knowing*. Why would you listen to someone if you think you already know what he or she has to say? When you treat your felt sense this way—for example, "I already know why I'm afraid"—you block your opportunity to find out what it's really about.

You might be asking, "But what if I do already know?" Let me say this: as long as there is still a felt sense wanting your attention, there is something about it you don't know yet. If you are still experiencing tightness, fear, constriction, or stuckness, there is something your body knows and is trying to tell you.

So be curious, open, and more interested in what you *don't* know yet than in what you already know. Try acknowledging what you already know about what you're Focusing on and then setting that aside. Not because it's wrong—it might not be—but because it might be getting in the way of sensing what is new and not yet known about you and your life.

Our modern culture puts a great premium on clarity. We are taught that if we can't think or say something clearly, then it's not important. The winner in school is the one who gets "the answer" the fastest—see those hands shoot up! It's rarely acknowledged that there is a valuable kind of knowing that is vague at first and takes time to access.

The bias for clarity can lead to feeling uncomfortable in the face of something unclear and unknown. "How would I explain this to anyone? How would I defend it? What good is it?" Before you learned to honor and listen to felt senses, you might have dismissed them in just this way.

Instead, enjoy them! When a felt sense first comes, you may not know what to call it, and you may not know what it is. Let that be OK. You will learn to delight in that not-knowing, to look eagerly for the parts of your experience that are not yet known, just as a treasure hunter is most excited by the treasure chests that have not yet been opened.

It may not seem likely that there would be wisdom hiding in this fuzzy, vague, hard-to-describe *something* that you feel in your body, but there is. That's exactly where the wisdom is: not in what is already clear and known—that's *old* information—but in what is *emerging* in you, the knowing that is coming into awareness right now. Learning Focusing is learning to value and even cherish the slow, subtle, and vague.

Following the felt sense

You can trust the felt sense to lead you to the center of the maze. It knows which way to go. All you have to do is follow and it will lead you right to the center. It wants to go there; it wants you to come, too. But only it knows the way, only it can take you there. To find your way, you need to trust it. You need to let go of controlling which direction you're going in. You have to let go of analyzing and asking why and judging.

You can try lots of things during the process that may be very helpful—but the *results* are beyond your control. You can't make the felt sense do anything it isn't ready and willing to do. You can't make it tell you anything, and you can't make it change—any more than you can make the shy animal your friend against its will. You can only try things and offer possibilities, respectfully and without expectations, and see what happens next. Trying to impose your will on the felt sense is an exercise in pure futility.

But trust and follow, and you will find that in the center of the maze lies the treasure you have been seeking.

Every Focusing session is unique

Remember that Focusing is a natural human process, and it is always more than we will be able to put into words. If there is one thing you can count on in Focusing, it's that you can't predict what is going to happen. Every time you sit down to do Focusing, especially at first, you may need to remind yourself that what happened last time probably won't happen today. It might be similar; it might be very different. It might feel like skipping along the surface; it might feel like deep sea diving. You might have lots of images today. You might have lots of detail about your life. It might be peaceful and quiet. There might be lots of tears. But the felt sense will only bring you what you can deal with, and if you trust it and flow with it, you will find a natural resting place, a warm shore, a little closer to home.

Chapter Four

Let's Begin Focusing

Now you are ready to begin Focusing. In this chapter and the following one I will show you how to go through each stage of Focusing. Each stage has "Tips" to help with the most common questions and difficulties. Most of the stages are marked by phrases that you can say to yourself, such as "I'm sensing into my body." These phrases will be grouped together so you can glance down at them during your Focusing session and guide yourself through the process. However, every Focusing session is unique, and sometimes you will find yourself skipping stages or adding new ones, because that is what feels right to your felt sense. Bring with you the inner climate of safety and trust that you learned in the previous chapter, and you won't go wrong.

Once you know how, you will also be able to focus on your feet, with your eyes open, while you're taking a walk, doing the dishes, or even driving. But first, let's look at Focusing in a quiet place while sitting comfortably.

Getting ready

When you first practice Focusing, it's best to find a time and place without any distractions. Close the door, turn off the phone, ask someone to corral the kids—do whatever you need to do to get some quiet time for yourself. It's ideal to set aside half an hour, but if all you can find is ten minutes in your day, even that much is valuable.

It's better to sit, not lie down, because you don't want to fall asleep. But if your physical condition is such that you are only comfortable lying down, by all means do so.

Tips

- Make sure you are warm enough. After sitting for a while you may start to feel cool, so you might want to have a sweater or a blanket handy before you start.

- You don't have to sit still, or in any particular position. Focusing is not the same as meditation.

- You might want to have your Focusing journal with you. This is a notebook in which you can, if you wish, record what comes in your Focusing session.

"Which way today?"

When starting a Focusing session you have the choice to use the session to work on something that you consciously select or wait and see what wants your attention now. Settle down, take a few deep breaths, and simply wonder if there is something specific you want to spend time with in today's Focusing session. The alternative is to just wait and see what comes.

Tips

- The kinds of issues you might choose to work on could be a decision, an unwanted habit, a reaction to someone or something (an object, an event), a physical symptom, or something you want more of in your life. Chapter Seven includes examples of many of these.

- You can also choose to return to something that came up in an earlier Focusing session.

- Sometimes when we become quiet enough to do Focusing, we find that there are things still "chasing" us. Or we remember an important chore we need to do. You might want to have a pencil and paper handy to jot down whatever is on your mind and getting in the way, so you'll be able to let it go for now.

"I'm sensing into my body."

Notice what you need to do to be reasonably comfortable. You might want to loosen your clothing, especially anything around your waist, and perhaps take off your shoes. Take some deep, relaxing breaths. Usually you will let your eyes close or gaze downward without looking at anything in particular. Notice the parts of you that are touching the chair or floor, and notice the feeling of being held up by what you're sitting on. Notice how your feet feel, how your hands feel, how your shoulders feel. Take time to be aware of yourself as a physical being, taking up space in the world, having weight and volume and substance.

After you feel that your awareness is in your body, bring your awareness into the middle area of your body, the part that includes your throat, chest, stomach, and abdomen. Take time to sense in your throat the same way you would check if you have a sore throat. You may feel clear there, or you may feel constriction, or potential tears, or something else.

Then bring awareness down inside your chest area. Be aware of anything, such as tightness, heaviness, constriction, expansion, blankness, or peacefulness. Then bring your awareness down into your stomach and abdomen area. Notice tightness, jumpiness, queasiness, blankness, peacefulness, or something else. If you feel nothing for the moment, it doesn't matter. At this point your body is like an empty stage, waiting for the curtain to go up. Next, we will invite the play to begin.

Tips

- If it is hard to bring your awareness into your body, take longer with this step. It might help to notice that you can feel where your arms and legs are without looking at them. This is called the "proprioceptive" sense, and it's a powerful sense we often take for granted. Try closing your eyes and lifting your arm in the air. Notice that you can tell where your arm is, as well as your fingers, your hand, your wrist.

You might experiment with feeling various parts of your body in this way.

- Another way of bringing your awareness into the middle of your body is to start with your feet and come up, like this: Wiggle a toe and sense what your toe feels like. Then move your awareness up into your knee, how does that feel? . . . And up into your hips, what's that like? . . . And now up into your abdomen and stomach. Just be there with your awareness. Don't worry if nothing seems to be happening. If this is at all strange or unfamiliar to you, then it is well worth practicing.

- If you are used to doing meditation or relaxation, you might need to be careful not to get too relaxed. You need to be able to remain aware of body sensations. If you are starting to drift off or are becoming so relaxed that you've lost awareness of your body, do something. Open your eyes for a moment, rub your hands together, stretch, move around a bit. Then bring your awareness back to your body again.

"What wants my awareness now?" or "How am I about that issue?"

Let your awareness rest gently in the middle area of your body: throat, chest, stomach, and abdomen. Imagine you are sending a welcoming invitation to your inner self. Say to yourself, in the middle of your body, "What wants my awareness now?" or "How am I about that issue?"

The first question is a general invitation, if you don't have a particular issue to work on. It's like saying to a friend, "I'm here. What would you like to talk about today?" The second question invites your body to give you its felt sense about the particular issue you chose to work on.

Now take time to notice how you are feeling in your body. You might notice sensations, emotions, or a kind of overall mood or atmosphere. It might feel different on different days, but you're just going to notice what it feels like today. There's no need to be too particular about what you're looking for; you're interested in anything that feels like *something*.

There may be something already there when you bring awareness into your body or, in response to your invitation, you may feel something beginning to form. Give it time.

When you are starting to become aware of something, and starting to sense where it is in your body, take time to notice what this something is like. What you notice might be unclear, slight, subtle, or vague, or it might be very strong and definite. Sense anything: an emotion like "sad" or "scared," a sensation like "tight" or "jittery," an image like "a knot" or "a rock"—anything at all.

Don't worry about whether what you are feeling is a felt sense. Just keep on sensing. How does it feel in your body? You might start to find a few words about it: "sad in my chest," "something kind of heavy in my stomach," "kind of jittery here," "an empty nothing," "a funny feeling about that decision I have to make." The list is endless. Each felt sense is unique.

Tips

- The biggest barrier to successfully finding a felt sense is wondering if you're doing it right—if you "really" have one. In fact, it might be a good idea at this stage to forget you ever heard the words "felt sense." We don't want the concept to get in the way of your experience. Just think of yourself as looking for "something." Anything can be something.

- Even nothing is something and can have its own quality: "a gray nothing," "a spacious nothing," "a tired nothing."

- Even if you have decided to work on a particular issue, your body might have other plans. There are two things that can happen. Either you can see if your body is willing to let you be with the issue you wanted to work with, or you can let go of that issue for today and go with what is wanting to have your attention. Either is fine.

- Felt senses can form in *any* part of your body, but generally are clearer and easier to work with in the middle area: throat, chest, stomach, and abdomen. Start by sensing in this middle area. But if your awareness is drawn to something in another area of your body, that's fine. Even physical symptoms can be felt senses, as we'll see in Chapter Seven.

- If feeling and expressing your emotions is familiar territory
for you, slow down a bit here. Focusing is not the same as
getting into your feelings, although it certainly includes feelings. If you feel sad, sense *where* in your body the "sad" is.
This takes a little time.

"I'm saying hello to what's here."

When you first become aware of something, say to it, "Hello. I know
you're there." Then take some time to notice how it responds to your
greeting. It might ease a bit, or settle like a bird on a branch, or feel
like someone getting comfortable to start a conversation, or it might
get clearer and stronger, as if coming into focus.

When you are saying hello, you are acknowledging that it's just
as it is. This can be a precious moment in the process as you experience yourself meeting this inner part of you. You are coming into
contact with what's true for you at this moment of your life. And that
always feels good, even if you don't like what you find.

Tips

- The most important thing is not to rush. Take your time
greeting your felt sense. Take time sensing how your body
feels as you do so.

- Saying hello is not only for the first thing you come in contact with. Each time you become aware of a new feeling or
part of yourself, say hello to it as well.

- Say hello literally, directly to it. Don't shout across a canyon
but come up to it, at the right distance for a good hello.

"I'm finding the best way to describe it."

After you say hello to your felt sense, the next step is to describe it.
Simply say to yourself how the sense feels right now in your body.
This is the same way you might tell another person how it feels in
your body right now. You'll usually use a word, a phrase, or an image.
It might even be a sound or a gesture. It's whatever gets closest to
describing how that sense feels right now.

A word, phrase, or image may already have come that starts to describe what you are aware of. (We gave the examples of "sad in my chest," "something kind of heavy in my stomach," "kind of jittery here," "an empty nothing," "a funny feeling about that decision I have to make.") Now is the time to let the description fill out until you start to feel you are getting to know this part of yourself more clearly. This is like getting to know its name.

This process of describing isn't something magical or strange. It's something we're all familiar with. If I had invented a new flavor for chewing gum and I gave you some to taste, you would put it in your mouth and chew on it for a while. Then if I asked you, "How would you describe that flavor?" you would roll it around in your mouth and say, "Um ... well, it's not exactly cinnamon ... it's not quite mint ... I know! It's ..."

Descriptions help you find your way to the center of the maze. You might know the descriptions you are finding are not quite right, but continuing to sense for good descriptions keeps you pointed toward the center. If something stirs, or moves, or gets stronger, or feels a little relieved as you become aware of this word or phrase or image, you are on the right track.

Continue to sense for just what description would fit this felt sense perfectly. "No, that's close but it's not *exactly* that. Let's feel that some more ... Yeah, it's more like this ..." When you find the description that fits your experience, you'll feel a satisfying sense of rightness. Several things might happen next.

You might feel the felt sense more strongly. This is a signal that you are moving toward the center of the maze. Follow that signal; you're getting closer.

You might feel a slight sense of relief. Usually this means that something has opened you weren't aware of before. Take a little time to receive that. It usually comes with a little insight into the whole issue. You're getting closer.

Finding the description might bring you right to the center of the maze. You will experience a distinct sense of release and relief. And as the body sensations ease, you might feel a spreading glow of warmth or peace. You might have a new insight about the whole thing: "Whew! So *that's* it! Now it makes sense." New steps might emerge. The whole thing might feel resolved and complete. You might want to end here. So just skip to the section in the next chapter called "I'm checking if it's OK to stop soon." And enjoy.

Tips

- You can't force a description onto the felt sense or force it to open. Even if you don't find a satisfactory word, phrase, image, or gesture, the very act of sensing for that as you are feeling this *something* in your body is of great benefit. So please don't strive and strain for a description. You might just want to remind yourself that gently wondering about it is more productive than pushing. Loving the felt sense is more important than understanding it. Understanding will come in its own time.

- The most important thing is to stay in contact with how it feels in your body. It's too easy to get caught up searching for the right word and lose touch with how your body feels. Every time you become aware that your attention has drifted from how you feel inside, just bring your awareness back to the inner area of your body. You might want to repeat to yourself the last description that felt close or brought some response.

- It can be helpful to write in your Focusing journal the descriptions that come at this stage. Then if you lose your place, you can look at the journal and repeat the descriptions to yourself as a way of getting back in touch with where you were.

"I'm checking back with my body."

Checking back with your body is more than a stage in the Focusing process. It is something you do over and over, all through the session. At this point, when you're finding the description, do it first. But then please continue.

Any words, sentences, images, or ideas that come *from* the felt sense need to be offered *back* to the felt sense for confirmation. This is a very powerful and important part of the process. Checking back with your body will move the session forward in a very deep and centered way. Here's how it works: You're feeling *something* in your body. Let's say it's in your throat. At first you can find no name for it; "something" is as close as you can get. You stay with it, and after a while you begin to feel you could call it "squeezing."

Now, take the word "squeezing" and offer it back to the feeling in your throat, as if you're saying, "Squeezing? Is 'squeezing' right?"

Three things may happen, and any of them will move the session forward. First, you may feel an inner sense of rightness. Yes, "squeezing" is just right, and there is a satisfying sense of having captured the essence of what is there. You'll be able to stay with the feeling more easily now, and go into the next stages (which we'll learn about in the next chapter).

Second, you may feel that that's partly right, but there's more. Yes, "squeezing" is part of it, but it's also something more . . . what? um . . . "scared"? Then you offer the word "scared" to the sense as well, and see if "squeezing and scared" is right.

Third, you may feel that "squeezing" is not right. But that's good too, because your sense of not right can lead you closer to what *would* be right. "Not 'squeezing' . . . it's more . . . um . . . Yes! Constriction!" And now you offer "constriction" to the sense, and feel for the inner sense of rightness there.

Later in the session, as whole sentences come, continue to offer them back to the body to check for their rightness, and sense (1) yes, that's right, (2) partly, but there's more, or (3) not right—and what *would* be right? This will be a powerful aid to your Focusing process.

Stop now, and before you read any further, try doing Focusing up to this point. If you're like many readers of self-help books, you tend to read the exercises and think about what might happen if you did them, instead of actually doing them. This is fine, but my intention is for you to *have* this skill. To have it, you must do it. So please start giving yourself practice by going through the stages as we've described them so far. Here they are, repeated:

- "Which way today?"

- "I'm sensing into my body."

- "What wants my awareness now?" or "How am I about that issue?"

- "I'm saying hello to what's here."

- "I'm finding the best way to describe it."

- "I'm checking back with my body."

Chapter Five

Deeper into Focusing

Now that you have learned how to bring awareness into your body and find *something* that wants to communicate with you, it's time to have the rest of the conversation. Up to this point, Focusing is like being introduced to someone and finding out their name. "Hello, you're tightness? Pleased to meet you." Now you are going to sit down with this inner part and learn its story, hear what it wants to tell you.

"Is it OK to just be with this right now?"

If you want to have a good and productive conversation, first you need to really be with the person you're talking to. You need to look them in the eye, say hello, make sure you have their name right—and then be there.

You are not in a hurry, you are not pushy, you are not trying to impose your own agenda on this inner part of you that wants your attention. You are just being there, being with it.

Take a nice, deep breath, settle into your body even deeper, and remind yourself that this is a process of spending time with something inside, just keeping it company.

"I'm sitting with it, with interested curiosity."

Next imagine that you are sitting with this something. I like the metaphor of sitting because it lets my body know that I'm not in a hurry. If you're having a conversation with someone but you're standing up, how patient can you be? Standing communicates that you are only taking a little time for this conversation, and soon you must be getting on to something more important. But if you sit down, you are giving the message that it's fine for this conversation to take some time.

The other important factor about the metaphor of *sitting with* is that you are not *in* the feeling, you are *with* it. (See the section on "Being in a relationship with your feelings" in Chapter Three.) Focusing is not about feeling as intensely as possible. Focusing is about keeping your feelings company so they can give their messages. This can be done best from the position of *next to* rather than *in*.

Next add a little respectful curiosity and interest. Without expectation, simply wonder if more is there. Sometimes I say to people at this stage, "Just sit with that place, like you'd sit with a friend. Gradually you may begin to sense something more, something you haven't put into words yet."

What comes at this stage might be very small: not the complete answer, just a little bit more. If it started out feeling "squeezed," in a little while it might feel "squeezed and resentful." Don't worry that you don't know yet what it's resentful about. What you don't know will always be bigger than what you know! Concentrate on what you do know. "Ah, resentful. OK, yes, squeezed and resentful. Let me just feel that much, for a while. . . . And is there more?"

This attitude is one of interested curiosity. I love the word "curiosity," because I find it very hard to imagine "judgmental curiosity"! Curiosity can be the openness and wonder of a child investigating the world. "Ah, what's this?"

Tips

- Felt senses can be very sensitive to pressure. Remember the shy animal at the edge of the woods. If your felt sense tends to disappear when you go to sit with it, this might be a sign that some part of you is not ready to allow it to be as it is. You might say hello to that part of you.

- Often we assume we know what something is, or what it feels like, because we described it once. For example, we may continue to call a sensation in the stomach "fear" when it has actually turned into excitement. It's important to continue to sense throughout the session if what has come *now* feels like a good fit to your felt sense, to ask of a description as you become aware of it, "Is this right?" and then if it doesn't fit, to sense for what is right.

- Did you say hello? Did you find a fitting description? Did you ask if it was OK to spend some time with this? The biggest reason for difficulty at this stage is skipping over the previous stages.

- Whenever you are feeling doubtful about what came, let that be a signal that it's time to check with your body. Even when you don't feel doubt, do check whenever something new comes from the sense. Checking helps you stay grounded in your body. It helps you notice subtle differences or changes that may be very important. Checking gives you practice in using and honoring your inner sense of rightness. It develops a trusting inner relationship with your body and your felt senses. Your body will feel that you're listening when you carefully check with it, and you will feel grounded and certain about what is there.

"I'm sensing how it feels from its point of view."

So far we have been approaching the felt sense from our point of view, from outside, so to speak. Now see if you can sense how the felt sense feels, from *its* point of view. If it sounds strange to talk about your felt sense having a point of view separate from your point of view, I assure you that this is quite possible and very productive.

Consider my student Jeanne. I asked her how it felt in her throat, and she said, making a face, "It feels uncomfortable." Can you tell whose point of view that was? Jeanne's, of course. Then I said to her, "OK, it feels uncomfortable. And could you also sense how *it* feels, from *its* point of view?" She was silent a moment, and then said, "Oh! *It* feels scared."

The difference between "It feels uncomfortable (to me)" and "*It feels scared*" is a very important difference. When you can make that inner shift, from sensing how the felt sense feels to you, to sensing how *it* feels, itself, you are well on the way to hearing your body's message and receiving its wisdom.

You know the way you can sense how a friend is feeling, even if he doesn't feel like talking. In that same way, you can sense more about this whatever-it-is inside you, without it "talking." You can sense its mood, perhaps, or a quality, or an atmosphere. Words may pop into your head, or an image, or a memory. You may visualize the sense in a posture, such as hiding or ready to fight. Be open to whatever comes to you.

Tips

- If nothing happens, back up and slow down! The most likely difficulty is that you are pushing too hard, expecting too much. See if you can hold the attitude that you are primarily building a trusting relationship with the inner senses in your body. Any information that may come is extra. Be there . . . *and* be interested.

"I'm asking . . . "

After you have spent some time with the felt sense, you might sense if it feels right to ask it a question. Sometimes a question can be very helpful. It can be a good way to remind yourself to stay with the body sense. A question gives the felt sense some gentle structure. It helps direct your attention to what *more* is there. At other times, questions don't feel right. The inside place doesn't want a question right now.

When you ask the felt sense a question, don't expect it to answer in a literal sense. Ask a question as a way of directing your awareness to sense more of what's there. When I first learned Focusing, asking questions was a problem for me. I kept thinking my inner place was supposed to open up a little mouth and talk back to me! When that didn't happen, I figured I was hopeless as a Focuser. Then I realized that, even for the people who were Focusing successfully, that wasn't what was happening for them. Little mouths weren't opening up inside them. Instead, they seemed to be sensing more, in response to holding an open, questioning attitude. Asking questions wasn't essential. What was essential was an attitude of friendly interest and respectful curiosity. So the purpose of the question is to help you hold the attitude.

I will give you the four most frequently helpful questions. But you and your process are unique, so be open to the possibility that, today, some other question might be the most helpful for you, and ask your body to help you sense what that question is.

"I'm asking if it has an emotional quality." If you haven't yet sensed any emotion, try asking at this point what emotion the felt sense has. For example, if the felt sense is "tightness," you might ask inwardly, "What is the emotional quality of this tightness?" You might try out a few possibilities: "Is it a scared tightness? Is it a joyous tightness? Is it an angry tightness?" Even if all the possibilities you suggest are wrong, as you say them keep sensing in your body, and it will let you know which emotion words are closer.

Once you are in contact with "scared tightness" or "angry tightness," there is a depth and a richness to your felt sense. You have a much better chance of learning even more than when you had just "tightness."

"I'm asking it, 'What gets it so _____?'" If your Focusing process needs another question, try using the description or the emotion word as part of the question:

"What gets it so _____?" Fill in the blank with the description you got earlier, or the emotion word from the previous question.

For example, if the description is "jumpy," you would ask the felt sense, "What gets you so jumpy?" Or if the emotion word is "scared," you would ask, "What gets you so scared?"

If what you're feeling seems obvious, as in "Of course, anyone would feel this way," try asking what feels the *most* that way. For example:

"What's gets you the most jumpy?"
"What's gets you the most scared?"

Remember, you haven't really heard the message of your felt sense until you hear something that you didn't already know.

"I'm asking it what it needs." If you've spent time with these questions and something still feels unfinished, try asking the felt sense: "Do you need something from me (or from the world)?" or

"What needs to happen next?" You wouldn't ask this kind of question first, because that's too much like trying to alleviate the feeling before you've heard its message.

What kind of presence does this place need? Does it just need my quiet company? Does it need some love and empathy? Does it need some encouragement to say more? Ask . . . and wait.

"I'm asking my body to show me how 'all OK' would feel." If you've asked all these questions and you still feel the need of something more, there is an additional type of question that can be quite magical. Someday, in some possible future, this whole thing, whatever it is, will be "all OK." In other words, the situation will be cleared up, resolved satisfactorily. The amazing thing is that your body knows *now* how it would feel to have the situation resolved, even though your logical mind has no idea how that could happen. So ask in your body, "How would 'all OK' feel right now?" and just wait. Let your body show you. Don't go with thoughts, such as "I think I would feel relieved," or "I'd probably be able to relax then." Ask your body to *show you* by beginning to feel that way right now.

This kind of question helps create a welcome for new ways of being and new action steps. Sometimes these steps arise spontaneously, but we can also invite them to form. It is important at this stage to sit back, wait, and see what comes from the felt sense. I promise you that what the felt sense can create is infinitely better, more creative, and richer than anything your conscious mind can think up. *You* may feel stuck, but *it* isn't!

Tips

- Remember, asking questions of the felt sense comes after saying hello to the felt sense, describing it, and seeing if it's OK to just be with it. The most common reason for getting nothing in answer to an inner question is that it was asked too soon. You need to establish a good relationship before something inside you will be *willing* to answer questions.

- If asking a question feels like an intrusion to your felt sense, check if you asked with an attitude of impatience, such as "Hurry up and tell me what you're about, right now!" If so, you'll need to say hello to that part of you that is impatient, and sit with that part, with interested curiosity, perhaps asking "What gets you so impatient?"

- There are many questions you could use to help your felt sense open up to you. You could ask if there is an image that would somehow express this whole thing. Or you might wonder what it is in your life that is bringing this feeling now. Or you might ask, "Where is the edge? Where is the boundary between what I know and don't know about this? What do I *almost* know." Or you can ask the felt sense, "What do you want me to know?"

- Don't ask any question that starts with the word "why." "Why" belongs to your logical mind, and your logical mind will happily leap in and take over. "Why" also contains a connotation of criticism or judgment (as in "Why are you holding the book that way?"). If you really want to ask a "why" question, try rephrasing it with "what." "Why are you angry?" becomes "What gets you so angry?" "Why are you hurting?" becomes "What happened that you're hurting?"

- Another sign of your logical mind taking over is if you find yourself saying "I think," or "probably," or "it must be." These are indications that the answer is not coming from the felt sense. Bring your awareness back to your body and ask the question again, or take the "logical" answer and ask the body, "Is this right?" You will learn to recognize the body's inner sense of rightness.

- The body takes time to answer. It is slower than our rational mind or our capacity to visualize. Answers that come quickly need to be confirmed with the body. They may be right, but we need to let the body tell us so.

- If you feel uncertain about whether what came is real, check with your body, with your felt sense. Ask it confirming questions, such as "Is this right? Have I understood you?"

- Sometimes no questions are needed. You don't have to ask questions. Be sensitive to what the felt sense needs. Questions are not to satisfy our curiosity, they are to help the felt sense express what it needs to let us know.

"I'm checking if it's OK to stop soon."

To end your Focusing session, first respectfully ask your felt sense if *it* feels OK about stopping. Ask it, "Is it OK to stop in a minute or two, or is there something more you need to let me know first?" This is not the same as asking if the problem is resolved. The problem may not be resolved, and it may certainly not be resolved in a way that your logical mind had expected. But it might still be time to stop. The feeling might be, "That's enough for now."

It's good to ask if something more needs to come and be known before you stop. Often the felt sense reveals something very important when it is asked that question. There have been times when people have felt this to be the most important part of the session.

Since change in Focusing comes in steps, a little more each time, your body may feel that this is enough for now, even though you can also tell—and it can tell you—that there is more to come at a later time.

The ending is a good time to review what came and to ask yourself what you would like to remember from the session. Focusing happens at such a deep level that your new awareness may tend to slip out of your consciousness unless you take a little time to remember. This is also a good time to receive fully any changes that may have happened. Even little changes need to be fully welcomed. And if a felt sense has transformed from something uncomfortable into a warm, spacious, pleasant, even glowing feeling, take the time to let that be there as much as it would like to be. Invite it to fill your body as fully as it wants to. This feeling doesn't have to stop just because your session is stopping; you can bring it with you!

Tips

- Even if you have time constraints, you can end a session gently. When you begin a session, let your body know how much time you have or when you need to stop: "We have ten minutes," or "I need to be getting ready for work by 7:00." The body has an amazing capacity for self-timing and will bring up something appropriate for that amount of time.

- Make sure that you start stopping a few minutes before you really have to stop. Barbara McGavin offers the rule of thumb that you generally need one to two minutes stopping time for every ten minutes of Focusing. So if you have a ten-minute session you'll probably need two minutes to stop, and if you have a thirty-minute session you'll probably need five minutes to stop.

- The Focusing process has a natural rhythm, a cadence of exploration and then rest. Usually there is a time about every five to ten minutes when it would be possible to stop, so you're never very far from a comfortable stopping place.

- The stages we have listed here are only suggestions. You don't have to go through them all (except that the earlier ones are important to help the later ones go well). Ending the session might feel right at any stage. Let your body tell you when ending is right; you don't have to focus for twenty minutes if it feels right to stop after fifteen.

"I'm saying, 'I'll be back.'"

You will be able to come back to your body later and continue this process. The most respectful leavetaking involves telling the inside place that you will be back. You're letting your body know you understand that this is part of a larger process, and there will be more.

Tips

- If something is not finished, at first the felt sense may find it difficult to let you go. It finally has your attention and may be afraid you won't come back. You may need to reassure it that you really will come back, and then, of course, you will need to keep your promise. Over time, as you show yourself to be trustworthy in this, your felt senses will find it easier to let you go at the end of each session.

- You might want to "mark the place." This is like using a bookmark to easily find your place again. There might be a vivid image, or a certain sentence or phrase, that will help you recall the place you reached. You might want to draw or write this in your Focusing journal.

"I'm thanking my body and the parts that have been with me."

This is also a time to thank and appreciate your body process for what it has given you.

Remember that the essence of Focusing is to have a good relationship with your inner self. You have succeeded in Focusing if you have stayed with something you feel in your body, even if nothing else happened. Congratulate yourself!

Summary of Focusing Phrases

- "Which way today?"

- "I'm sensing into my body."

- "What wants my awareness now?" or "How am I about that issue?"

- "I'm saying hello to what's here."

- "I'm finding the best way to describe it."

- "I'm checking back with my body."

- "Is it OK to just be with this right now?"

- "I'm sitting with it, with interested curiosity."

- "I'm sensing how it feels from its point of view."

- "I'm asking if it has an emotional quality."

- "I'm asking it, 'What gets it so _____?'" [emotion or description word]

- "I'm asking it what it needs."

- "I'm asking my body to show me how 'all OK' would feel."

- "I'm checking if it's OK to stop soon."

- "I'm saying, 'I'll be back.'"

- "I'm thanking my body and the parts that have been with me."

Chapter Six

Receiving the Gifts

The positive feeling that comes from Focusing is such a special experience that I'd like to take time to tell you about how to receive it. Gendlin calls this positive feeling the "felt shift." It is a time when everything in your body/mind, in your whole organism, is rearranging itself to accommodate the new understanding you have received.

In other methods, you may have to take it on faith that something good has happened. But in Focusing, your body tells you immediately that something fundamental has changed, and it tells you by feeling good in a rather special way. You will probably recognize this feeling. It will probably be familiar from times in your life when you felt a kind of "aha!" after puzzling out a difficult problem. Or you may have this kind of feeling when you are in the flow of a creative project, at those moments when everything clicks into place. It feels marvelous.

The felt shift feels like fresh air coming into a closed room, or new life awakening and stirring inside, or excitement, or energy moving. There may be a distinct sense of relief and release. Often people feel clarity, peace, and groundedness; a warm, spacious well-being.

When this happens (and it could be at any time in the session), give yourself some time to receive this gift. We have such a tendency to rush on, to *do* something with what came, or to figure it out, or to get back to work on the rest of the problem, or on another problem. We treat our problems like patients in a waiting room. When one is eased a little, we call out "Next!" Instead, remind yourself to simply welcome what came . . . make room for it . . . receive it. Take time to feel how it feels.

When your session stops, the good feeling doesn't have to stop. Feel free to bring it back with you. Invite it to fill your body as much as it wants to. It might even expand beyond the boundaries of your body.

If you don't feel better after Focusing

What if you don't feel good? Did Focusing fail?

Probably not. Remember that Focusing involves *building a relationship* with your inner self. Relationships always take time to build. If you haven't spent much time with your felt senses before, they may need some time to come to trust you. Each Focusing session is a part of building that trust. Each session builds on the one before.

Large life issues (the ones we most want to change!) will need several sessions. You may need to return to something over days, weeks, or even months. (And not every session has to be about that issue.) You may feel the steps of change long before an issue feels resolved. A step of change is like: "OK, at least I know *this* much. Yes, it feels good and right so far. And I can stop for now and come back to this later."

Focusing usually feels good. How good it feels depends on a lot of factors. Be sure to welcome *any* good feeling, like a gardener who is glad when a green shoot first shows above the ground, long before it becomes a flower.

Grounding a transformative session

Occasionally, especially after you have been Focusing on something over a number of sessions, you will have a session that feels *really* good. You feel transformed, released, a big shift. Everything about this issue feels different. In this case it is vitally important to ground the session. You really have changed, but for a time your old habit patterns will co-exist with the new. Imagine yourself in situations where the old pattern was found, and notice how you feel now, and how you behave now. Most important is to sense how your body feels *now,* to feel how your body has changed. Stay with that changed feeling until it feels like it has settled into the very tissues and bones of your body. Don't just open your eyes and go about your day as if nothing had happened. That will make it harder for the new, transformed way of being to begin to operate in your life. Instead, if you can, take some extra time after the session to honor what happened.

Write about it in your Focusing journal. Sit for a while, just feeling, and then write. Begin with what you are feeling now, in your body. Then tell the story of the session, as much as you remember. How you started, what came next, what came after that. Especially write down what it was that came directly before your shift in feeling. Perhaps it was a sentence, such as "I am enough." Perhaps it was a symbol, or an image, such as a tree with spreading branches and roots going deep in the ground. After writing, sit quietly again, sensing if any more needs to be written to capture how you feel now.

Create art or music afterward. If you draw or paint, play an instrument or sing, or write poetry, you might want to create something after your transformative session. Unlike writing in your journal, this creation does not have to tell the story of your session, unless you want it to. Free yourself of any constraint about what it should be, and just create what comes. Set aside all judgment about whether you are "good" at this; your creation is for you, not to show to others (unless you want to, of course). Then come back to it later, and physically re-experience your own creation as you read, hear, or see it.

Tell a friend what happened. Find a trusted friend, soon after your transformative session, and tell him or her what happened. Tell your friend that you would like him or her to listen without suggestions or advice. As you tell, let your body re-experience what happened in the session as much as feels appropriate.

Positive feelings can support a physical healing process

Focusing can enable you to access your body's powers of physical healing, and this can be a very powerful and positive experience.

My friend Chris Rex was dealing with her second breast cancer in seven years. The night before her operation, she did Focusing to help prepare herself. She assumed the Focusing session would be about her fears about the operation and her anxiety about its success.

She sat down to do Focusing and brought her awareness into her body. Almost immediately, she was surprised by strongly pleasurable feelings of energy running through her arms and legs and into the trunk of her body. The thought came to her, "This is healing energy," and tears of joy came to her eyes.

The next day, as she was in the hospital preparing for the operation, she could feel her confidence in her body's healing power. She was smiling as she rolled into the operating room. The operation was a success, and her body healed quickly.

A few months later she was in radiation therapy and was having a hard time. Once again she did Focusing, expecting to get in touch with fear and resentment at having her skin burned in order to prevent the return of her cancer. But this time when she brought awareness into her body, she had the image of a cooling waterfall. She felt a healing coolness all through her body, including the burned area. Her radiation therapy became much easier to take.

Treasure your new good feelings, no matter how small

Powerfully transformative sessions are wonderful, but most sessions will feel good in a milder way. Just as the felt sense can be vague at first, and not very strong, so can the felt shift. Be sure to accept it, and celebrate it, just as it is.

What has come in you is like a new green shoot, and now *you* are the gardener. It's your job to protect that new green shoot from the voice that says, "That's not enough!" and from all the other critical voices. It's painfully easy to discount the new steps of change that come in a Focusing session. Just the other day a student said to me, shaking his head, "I have no guarantee that this works or is valuable other than the fact that I feel better after every session."

And don't worry about whether you understand what happened. You can expect some times when your body feels different but your mind doesn't yet understand. So let your mind take a rest, especially during this time, and just protect, receive, and welcome. Be the gardener, and remember that when the new green shoot first comes up in the garden, it isn't good for anything yet, and that's OK!

Chapter Seven

Specific Uses of Focusing

In this chapter I'd like to offer you some stories about people using Focusing for particular purposes. This will be a chance to see how Focusing actually works in practice. Because Focusing is a very broad purpose skill these examples don't cover all the possibilities, but they do suggest how Focusing can be applied to situations that arise in our lives.

Dealing with overwhelming feelings

After her marriage broke up, Mary often found herself in tears. She felt fragile, as if she might fall apart at the least touch. She feared her friends would become tired of her neediness, and she tried to push her feelings away.

She hoped Focusing would help, but at first it seemed to make things worse. "When I put my awareness in my body," she said, "I feel the tears filling up my throat and my chest, and I feel scared that it's just too much."

Then she remembered the Focusing step of acknowledging by saying hello to what is there. She said hello to the tears and hello to the part of her that was scared. She was surprised to notice a feeling of relief. The tears were still there, but they seemed to be at a slight distance, not threatening to overwhelm her.

"Before," said Mary, "the tears were like big ocean waves, and I was drowning. Now the tears are more like a lake. It's a big lake, but I'm just standing next to it. It's amazing, but I just don't have to get into that lake."

By acknowledging, by saying hello, Mary found a more comfortable relationship with her feelings. Now, for the first time, she could listen to her tears, because she was centered enough to be able to listen.

"Hello, tears," she whispered. "Is there something you want to tell me?"

Then she waited, just feeling in her body, in her throat and chest. It was like asking a question of a sad friend and then waiting patiently for the friend to speak.

As she waited, she began to get the impression of a child, a young girl about four years old. The girl was looking at her with big, sad eyes. Mary had the feeling that the girl was saying to her, "Please don't abandon me again!"

Mary was puzzled, so she said to the girl, "OK, but tell me, when did I abandon you?"

Again she waited, and slowly she began to see scenes from her marriage, times when she had put her own feelings and needs aside because she thought she had to put her husband first. Now she could see the little girl in those scenes, standing at the edge of the room, like a ghost, her own feelings and needs waiting hopelessly to be noticed.

She started to cry, but this time the tears felt welcome and fresh, not overwhelming. She spoke to the little girl, and felt the inner strength in her body as she said, "I won't abandon you again! I won't abandon you again!"

Overwhelming feelings are a signal that something very important is wanting to have our attention, wanting to be heard. Unfortunately the very intensity of the feeling may interfere with our willingness to hear it. When we can start by saying hello and forming a positive relationship with the feeling, it becomes easier to bear, and it is able to give its message.

Although tears may sometimes accompany an overwhelming feeling, they may also feel welcome and fresh, a sign that something true and important is being felt. Your body knows the difference.

Releasing an addiction

Angela worked with me to change her habit of eating too many sweets. She didn't realize that in the process she would also release herself from her dead-end job, which she hated.

She sat quietly and brought her awareness into the middle area of her body. She was inviting the part of her that liked to eat sweets to communicate with her. Soon she began to feel something in her solar plexus area. I encouraged her to take her time to feel it and describe it.

"It feels like grief," she said. "But I don't know what it's about." I invited her to stay with the feeling in a gentle, compassionate way, and notice anything more she might be aware of about that place. Soon she added, "There's a hole. There's a part of me that's grieving, and keeps trying to fill that hole."

I asked her to keep on sensing that place in her body, and to send it empathy, trying to sense how it felt from its point of view.

"It's grieving because it doesn't want to change; this is all that it has known."

I suggested that she acknowledge this. When she did, she was aware of more: "Now there's fear . . ." She was feeling the fear in the same place, the solar plexus area of her body.

"It's something about feeling good," she said. She was quiet for a few moments, sensing more. "This part of me gets scared when I feel good too long, so it comes in and binges. Oh! It's been protecting me! At least, it thinks it's protecting me."

This was a big realization, and Angela's voice had softened quite a bit. She was feeling the difference in her body, too, a sense of warmth and compassion for this part of her. The fear was still there, but it had lightened.

"I'm feeling a lot of compassion for this part," she reported. "It's had to be afraid for so long."

Then a connection with her job came. "Oh! This part is afraid of feeling joy, so it keeps me in a job where I don't feel any." She continued to sense that area of her body, aware of the inner meaning coming there. "This part believes where there's joy, there's pain."

Now even I could sense a difference. She seemed to be glowing with an inner light. "It's like a great big dam has just let go. There's energy flowing through me now. It's like being lifted out of a cave, to where you can see and smell and hear again."

I asked her how that place in her body felt now. "It feels loving and joyful and free," she reported.

Three months after her session, Angela was in a training program for a new career that brought her joy. Her eating of sweets was moderate and not a problem.

When using Focusing with an addiction (any repetitive behavior that interferes with our being fully present to our feelings), invite a felt sense of the part of you that *wants* to do the behavior. This is the part that wants to eat sweets, the part that wants to drink, the part that wants to smoke. This part has not had a voice because you have been to busy condemning it ("It's not healthy to drink so much") or excusing it ("But I deserve a little relaxation in my stressful life"). Focusing allows you to sense from *its* point of view and to discover the underlying purposes that this part of you is pursuing.

It may also be productive to ask if there is another part which is being hidden or suppressed by the addictive behavior. You can ask yourself in your body, "Is there something hidden under this?" Another powerful question is, "Is there something that wants to live?"

Making a decision

Matt was living in Chicago but he felt an urge to live elsewhere. An important relationship had recently ended, and his job wasn't what he really wanted to do. His best friend had moved to Seattle and was enjoying the city a lot. Matt visited Bob for a week and got a taste of life in Seattle. But he found it hard to decide to move. He had lived in Chicago a long time and had a network of friends and a comfortable home.

He tried making a list of the pros and cons of moving and staying. There were advantages and disadvantages to both moving and staying, and after Matt made the lists he felt as uncertain as ever. So he decided to try Focusing.

When Focusing on a decision that has two clear options, it is often best to take one option at a time and get a felt sense of each one separately. Matt first chose the option of staying in Chicago. He brought his awareness into his body, and pictured himself staying in Chicago. He asked his body for a sense of that: "How does staying in Chicago feel in my body?"

He waited, and in a few moments he began to notice a heavy feeling, especially in his arms and legs. In his stomach and abdomen there was something hard to describe. He stayed with the feeling in his stomach and abdomen, and got the word, "Stagnant." He checked that word back with his body: yes, stagnant was right. He asked if it would be OK to sit with that stagnant feeling, to sense how *it* felt from *its* point of view. In a few moments he got the words, "Going nowhere." He checked with his body, and that was right: staying in Chicago felt like going nowhere.

Matt felt complete with that option, so he thanked that body feeling and set it aside. Then he pictured himself moving to Seattle. He asked, "How does moving to Seattle feel in my body?"

This time he felt a tingling excitement in his arms and legs. He felt a lightness through the whole middle of his body, especially his chest. He checked the word "lightness" and found that it felt right. When he stayed with that feeling, the words came, "moving forward." Matt ended his session with a clear sense that moving to Seattle felt like moving forward.

Matt continued to think about his decision. He researched jobs in Seattle and talked to friends. He focused several more times, with similar results. After about a month he gave notice at his job, packed up, and moved to Seattle. Within a week he met someone, and a year later he was living with her happily. A job was harder to find, but he never regretted his move.

Most people find that one Focusing session is not enough for making a decision as big as a move to a new city. This may take several sessions, over time, along with other factors such as researching the practical aspects of the decision. Focusing may also result in a sense that this may be the right decision, but the timing isn't right yet. Focusing can be a key part of any decision, especially a big decision, because you don't want to make an important decision with your logic alone! You want to bring your heart and your gut into it to be sure that all of you is satisfied with the choice.

Getting information from a physical symptom

Kay had no idea why she suddenly started sneezing all the time. It reminded her of an allergic sneeze, but nothing about her lifestyle or the weather conditions had changed recently. There were reasons why she did not want to take medication to suppress the sneezing, so her life was rather miserable. Sleep was especially difficult. She decided to use Focusing to see if she could understand the inner meaning of this physical symptom.

She brought her awareness to the middle area of her body and then moved her awareness to her head, saying hello to the feelings there. She realized that her eyes, nose, and ears were all involved, all sending signals of some kind. She found the word "scratchy" for the physical feel of all that. Then she sat with "scratchy" with gentle curiosity.

In a few minutes she got the words "tired" and "full up." She checked back with her body: yes, those words were right. Then she asked the feeling, "What area of my life does this feel connected with?" and in a moment she sensed, "My job."

After acknowledging that answer, she asked further, "What is it about my job that brings this scratchy, tired, full up feeling?" Images began to come to her: she was indirectly involved in a labor dispute, and she was having to put in longer hours in order to respond to complaints she felt were frivolous. "Is that it?" she asked her body, and there was a feeling: *that's part of it, but that's not the central issue.* So she waited, inviting the central issue to come into her awareness. She got the words, "It's about me not trusting *me.*" At that point she felt a big relief in her body, and her eyes and nose felt clear. She allowed herself to just enjoy that feeling, to savor it for a while.

But Kay was aware that her ears still had something more to tell her. So she brought awareness again to her ears, and once again looked for a word to name the physical feeling. The word that came was "aching." She checked "aching," and it was right. She sat with the aching feeling with an attitude of interested curiosity. She got the word "clamor," and it felt right, but not complete. In fact, "clamor" felt like a very good word to describe the work atmosphere these days! So she asked the feeling in her ears, "What is it about the clamor that feels so aching?"

Then she got it: "Oh! I need to listen to *my* inner voice!" Once again this brought relief, and an inner sense of rightness. She still felt a little aching in her ears, but it didn't feel as though there was more information there. It felt like the little aching was there to remind her of what she had learned.

As Kay ended the session by thanking her body, she realized she had been sitting for forty minutes without a single sneeze! The next day, however, her nose was running as much as before.

Quite often the information we get from a physical symptom is true, and feels right, but the physical symptom doesn't change. It's as if Focusing is only part of the picture at this level. On the other hand, sometimes physical symptoms do change as a result of Focusing. One night before a workshop, I came down with a sore throat. I was discouraged, because I hate being sick while teaching. My co-leader suggested that I focus on it. In my session, I discovered a part of me that was feeling stretched past its limits by new aspects of my work. I heard and acknowledged its feelings. Within an hour, the sore throat was gone.

Releasing writer's block

Releasing writer's block is my own story, one of the many successful times I have used Focusing in my own life, and certainly one of the most striking. This is not the story of one session, but of many. I will just give the highlights here, but the truth is that releasing my writer's block with Focusing happened over years. And it was worth it.

The first time I tried to use Focusing to release my writer's block, I brought my awareness into my body and tried to experience the felt sense of not being able to write. In my chest I got a feeling of darkness, hiding. Not writing felt like hiding. That was all.

In my next Focusing session on that issue, I asked again for the felt sense of the writer's block. Again it started with darkness and a feeling of hiding, but there was something more. After a few minutes I was able to articulate the subtle difference. It didn't just feel like hiding, it felt like *ducking*. If I stuck my head up, something was going to get me. Writing was like sticking my head up, and some part of me was scared of what would happen.

In my next session I started with the feeling of being scared to put my head up. I got an image of being on a shooting range—at the target end. If I showed myself, I'd be sniped at. The word "sniping" felt very important; I could feel changes in my body, heat expanding in my chest, as I got that word. I said it to myself, "sniping, sniping," and felt the body reaction. Then suddenly I got an image of my father's face with a sarcastic expression. In his voice I heard the words, "Who do you think you are?"

A flood of knowing came into my body/mind, all at once. I remembered how my father had sniped at me with sarcasm, especially when I expressed myself in an expansive way, which he called "showing off." I realized that the tender, creative parts of me had gone into hiding out of fear and protection against these attacks.

When I opened my eyes at the end of that session I felt different. My whole body felt new, fresh, open. I didn't know what was going to change, but I knew that something was; it was a whole new world out there.

And my writing changed. It wasn't completely easy, but it was easier. Focusing had helped me communicate with the part of myself that was in the way of writing. The act of communicating, of hearing how this part of me really felt, was enough to bring some release. For several years after the revelation about my father's "sniping" I got by, writing in bursts but procrastinating for periods of time in between. I was glad it was better, but impatient for more, especially since I had a taste of what it was like to write with ease. So I sat down to do Focusing again.

Once again I brought my awareness into my body and asked for the felt sense of the part of me that didn't want to write. I consciously set aside my impatience and invited an attitude of acceptance.

I began to sense a tight band across my chest. As I kept my awareness with this band, I began to sense its strength. It was strong and there was also something more, some quality I found hard to put words to. It was almost as if this feeling had life, a particular kind of life. It was brash, fresh, bursting with energy, but also stubborn, young. Finally I got it: this tight band felt "adolescent"! With that realization came a picture of me as an adolescent, hands on hips, saying, "You can't make me do it!"

Instead of arguing with this adolescent or trying to break her spirit, I admired her strength and appreciated her stubborn power. I spent time trying to listen to her, to sense what she was saying and what she needed. By the end of the Focusing session I felt I had acknowledged the inner yearnings of the part of me that didn't want to be pushed around by anyone.

I didn't know if anything would change in my life because of this session. True, I felt better afterwards, but no decisions were reached, no concessions made. The adolescent seemed as stubborn as ever. So I was taken by surprise by what happened the next day.

My writing time approached and I turned on my computer, expecting to feel the familiar reluctant drag away, the feeling of "Let's do anything but this." Instead I felt a strong positive energy pulling me *toward* the computer! And the quality of that positive energy was brash, fresh, stubborn, young—my adolescent! She was drawing me toward the computer; she was saying, "Come on, let's write!" The very energy that had blocked me was now totally on my side because its concerns and feelings had been heard. Since that time, I have never had any difficulty writing, and the difference in my life is like night and day.

Using Focusing with an action block is similar to using it with an addiction. An action block, like writer's block or procrastination, can be expressed as "I want to _____ , but I don't." In Focusing, you assume there is a part of you that *doesn't want* to do the behavior, and you invite a felt sense of that part of you, with an accepting attitude. This process gives a voice to something that has not had a voice and releases the blocked system, often in unexpected ways.

Be prepared to be surprised. As you sense this block in a new way, you may even discover that what you thought you wanted to do isn't really so. One woman worked on a block that stopped her from doing sports. ("I've had this block for ten years.") After Focusing with the part of her that didn't want to do sports, she announced, "I realize that I hate sports!" She then formulated a new goal: to be more active in vigorous body movement. She joined a dance class; no more block.

Getting clear on an interpersonal issue

Jan left a good job in order to go back to graduate school. When she heard her best friend was applying for the job she had left, she had a strong reaction. It wasn't that Jan had expected to go back to the job herself; she had given it up with no strings attached. But she felt "weird," as she put it, when she heard her friend was applying.

It bothered her for weeks, no matter how often she told herself it was unimportant, no big deal. She didn't get anywhere thinking about it either.

So she sat down to do Focusing. She brought her awareness into her body, especially into the middle of her body, and invited her body to give her the feeling connected with this issue.

In a minute or two, she began to feel something in her middle. At first it was so vague that the word "something" was the only way to describe it. Then she began to get that it was "kind of tight, kind of elongated." She checked those words with her body, and yes, they felt right. Then she stayed with the feeling.

In a while she began to sense sadness there. This came as a surprise; of all the feelings she had expected, sadness was not one of them. But she acknowledged the sadness, and stayed with it. Soon it began to feel right to ask it a question, so she asked it, "What is it that gets you so sad?"

In response to the question, she could feel that part of her tightening up and then spreading out again. She could feel that the sadness had something to do with being invalidated. But when she checked with her body if those words were right, they weren't.

"That's not it," she said to herself. "It's . . ." A long pause. "It's not being believed!"

A flood of memories came into her head of all the conversations she had had with her friend about how difficult her job was, what a tyrant the boss was. Jan realized some part of her felt that if her friend was trying for the job now . . . "It's like she didn't believe what I said!"

After this realization came a feeling of relief and the uneasy, weird feeling simply lifted. That was what it was, and there was no need to do anything about it now. Jan didn't even have to decide to let it go; it had already released, and in its place was a warm, comfortable, open feeling.

Forming a better relationship with the inner Critic

Darrell was starting a course of study that would lead to a new career, one that he felt would bring him more satisfaction and fulfill some of his lifelong goals. But he was over forty, and whenever he was about to take action in connection with his courses, such as calling the school to find out the class schedule, he heard an inner voice whispering "It's too late. You've wasted too much time already."

He tried to quiet this voice by telling himself it wasn't true, many people went back to school at his age. But the voice didn't stop, and the tension in his stomach got tighter. He told friends about his worries, and they responded by telling him the same things he was telling himself: "It's not too late! It's never too late." This did not help either.

So Darrell did Focusing with this issue. He sat down and brought his awareness into his body. Then he invited his body to give him the whole feel of going back to school. He became aware of a lot going on. There was not just one feeling, but two or three.

He asked himself, "What's first?" and sensed an excitement in his solar plexus area. He checked the word "excitement," and that was right. He said hello to the excitement, and it sharpened. It was as if it said, "Yes! I'm here!"

Then he asked, "OK, what else is here?" and waited. Slowly he began to sense a shyer feeling, hiding behind the excitement. The word that came was "hesitant." He checked the word "hesitant" with the feeling, and that was partly right. After a moment he also got the word "careful."

Darrell said hello to the hesitant, careful feeling. As he did, he heard his inner Critic saying, "You've already wasted too much time!" He said to himself, "There's *a part of me* that feels I've wasted too much time . . . and I'm saying hello to that, too." Instead of listening to what the voice was saying, he sensed its *feeling*. "Is it scared of something?" he asked. Yes, he felt fear tinged with sadness. "It's scared I might never get what I want." With this he felt a releasing in his body, an inner "Yes, that's right." So he acknowledged the fear. The inner Critic faded, and once again he felt both the excitement and the hesitant, careful feeling.

Then he asked himself if it felt right to stay with both feelings for a while, or if one feeling was drawing him more. It felt right to stay with both. It felt right that neither feeling would "win," or be more important than the other. So he stayed with both. He said to himself, "I'm letting both the excitement and the hesitant, careful feeling just be here right now."

At first he felt a sort of pulling back and forth, as if the two feelings were vying for his attention. But then there was a change. His breathing relaxed, and he felt a settling down in his body. He felt something new in the presence and the relationship of these two feelings, and after a moment he was able to put this into words. It was as if the excitement and the hesitant, careful feeling had become partners. They were like two pillars, one on each side of his body, holding him, giving him strength. One part held the wisdom of right timing, and the other part held the excitement of moving forward.

Under the image of the pillars, at the center of his body, he could feel his fear of not getting what he wanted from a career, and he could feel how it was soothed and supported by the two partners: the wisdom of right timing and the excitement of moving forward. He asked the fear what it wanted, and the answer was, "To really feel I'm using my talents to make a contribution to the world."

He asked his body to show him how it would feel if he *knew*, right now, that he would be able to use his talents to make a contribution to the world. In the center of his body a warm, expansive feeling began to spread, and grow. He invited it to be there as fully as it wanted to be, and spent the rest of his session enjoying and getting acquainted with the positive feelings that came.

The inner Critic is always afraid of something. You can disarm its attacks by asking, gently, "What are you afraid of?" After you have received the answer to that question, you can ask, "What do you want?" For more about the inner Critic see Chapter Eight.

Any fear can be asked what it wants. This allows you to feel the positive energy hidden inside the fear. "I'm afraid I'll be too tired" might become "I want to have energy." "I'm afraid people won't like my work" might become "I want my work to be appreciated." See if you can feel the difference between the two statements in each pair. Both may be true, but the second has a positive quality that allows forward movement. So first acknowledge fear, and then ask what it wants.

After you have sensed what the fear wants, ask your body to show you what it would like to have that desire fulfilled now, or what it would be like to know now that you will be able to have it fulfilled in the future. You might still be afraid, but now you can also feel the positive energy that comes from receiving what you want.

Chapter Eight

Troubleshooting

By now you've tried Focusing a few times. If it has been easy and productive for you, bless you! (You are unusual.) Most people encounter sticky spots as they rediscover this skill which revolutionizes our cultural training. This chapter will help you with some of the difficult places you might be encountering.

"I have a hard time getting a felt sense."

I remember when I was first learning Focusing there was an exercise in which we were instructed to bring our awareness into our bodies and notice what we felt. I was enormously frustrated. Nothing! I felt like I was a total blank. I didn't feel anything and I didn't know how to feel anything. I was ashamed of my inadequacy, depressed that I might never learn this, and anxious that the cute boy across the room might never want to focus with me. Feeling nothing, eh? As you can tell, I was actually feeling a lot! But I wasn't acknowledging my feelings. They weren't what I expected, or what I thought I was supposed to find, so they just didn't count.

If you try Focusing and get a blank, here are some helpful hints. Many of them have to do with including something you might have been ignoring.

Maybe you feel something positive. You might be diligently looking for tightness or heaviness, or something else uncomfortable or unpleasant, and go right past what is there: something positive, like peacefulness, expansiveness, openness, or warmth. Felt senses can feel good! If you're expecting to feel bad, you might think you feel "nothing," when actually you do feel something, but it's something good.

Ask yourself, in your body, "Do I possibly feel something positive?" "Do I feel wonderful in my body right now?" Then be open to *all* sensation—tight or relaxed, heavy or light, contracted or expanded. Notice if there's a difference between how your chest feels and how your stomach feels. Notice if your throat feels different from either your chest or your stomach. Sometimes it's possible to feel *differences* even when it's hard to say *what* the differences are.

Maybe you feel something subtle. Felt senses can be quite subtle. As inheritors of Western industrial culture, we haven't been taught to attend to subtle sensation. When I was growing up, you ignored your body as long as you could, and when you couldn't ignore it any more, you took a pill or went to the doctor. If our bodies have to shout to get our attention, they will do that. But wouldn't it be better to listen to our bodies while they're still whispering, before they have to shout?

It can take a while to learn to feel subtle sensation in the body. You need to tune your awareness down to that level. It's as if you took a person who's been listening to only loud music and seeing only bright colors, and set her down in a beautiful forest. At first she says, "Gee, it's boring here! Nothing is happening!" But in a little while, if she cares to, she begins to notice that something is happening, and that there *are* sounds. After a little longer she discovers that the forest is endlessly fascinating, but only after she has tuned her awareness to be able to sense what is going on there.

So when you try Focusing, be sure to be open to subtle sensation. Don't be like the person who told me that he felt nothing in an exercise. When I asked him to give me more detail about his experience, he said, "Well, first I felt sort of a little shaky feeling in my throat, but I decided it wasn't strong enough so I looked for something else. Then I felt what might possibly have been a tightness in my stomach, but it could just have been from the way I was sitting, so I looked for something else. Then I felt what might have been an expansive feeling in my heart area, but I decided I was probably just making that up because I'd like to feel that way. Then nothing more happened, so I opened my eyes, and told you I felt nothing!"

Give your felt senses the benefit of the doubt. If they *might* be there, assume they *are* there. And see what happens!

Maybe you feel something hard to describe. Your felt sense may be definitely there, but hard to put into words. Congratulate yourself! This is the experience that correlated with successful therapy in the research that led to the development of Focusing. People who felt something, but could not at first find the words to describe it, were the most likely to have successful outcomes in therapy.

It's really worth the time it takes to slowly find the words to fit the felt sense. Our culture does not teach us to honor the slow process of finding the right words for a vague sensation. There's a premium on speed and on being "articulate," which means having the words come quickly, whether or not they are true. Thus we betray ourselves by continually turning away from inner truth toward something easier to say, easier to explain.

If you feel something hard to describe, try using my favorite word "something" to acknowledge it. "I'm feeling *something*." This positive acknowledgment will make it easier to stay with what you are feeling, even if other descriptions are elusive. Then let yourself look for expressions like "kind of . . ." or "sort of . . ." or combinations of words like "sticky-furry" or "jumpy-nauseous-excited." Remember, it isn't finding the right description that matters, it's the *process* of inner attention.

"I can't focus on one thing; there are too many things going on."

There may be many things that want your attention today. It is as if you have walked into a room and everyone is shouting for your attention. If it feels like chaos when you bring your awareness into your body, you may want to do a Focusing process called "clearing a space."

In clearing a space you acknowledge each "something" as you become aware of it, without going into it. Say hello to each one, and imagine asking each one to find somewhere safe to be where you can find it again later. You might invite it to go outside of you, onto a shelf nearby, or a pillow in front of you. You might need to know a little about what it is, or take time to find an image or a descriptive word so that you can find your way back to it. You might even write each one briefly in your journal. Let each thing know that you are willing to come back and spend more time with it later. This helps it to let go of you. Keep asking, "What else needs to be acknowledged?" and repeat this process with each issue or feeling that comes.

Eventually—sooner than you'd think—you'll get to a place where nothing more comes in answer to a "What else?" question. You'll probably feel peaceful and spacious inside. If not, notice if there is a "background feeling." This is a feeling that is so constantly there, in the background, that we don't even notice it any more. It's like the wallpaper—how often do you notice the color of your own wallpaper? It has become normal to feel "always tired," or "always pushing," or "always sad," or "always" something else. Notice if there is something like this for you. Then ask that, too, to find somewhere safe to go, outside of you.

The most common difficulty in clearing a space is getting into a struggle with your feelings, trying to get them to go out onto that shelf when they don't want to. They have to let go of you voluntarily. You can invite; you can't force. If something keeps clinging to you, try asking it, "What do you need right now so that you can wait a while for my attention?"

"Does Focusing have to be about problems? What if I'm feeling good?"

Focusing does not have to be about problems. You can have very rich and productive Focusing sessions starting with felt senses that feel good, like feeling relaxed, warm, open, peaceful, expansive, and so on. When you are noticing how your body feels at the beginning of the session, be sure to include positive feelings. Don't ignore them as nothing. They're not!

Treat these positive feelings as you would any felt sense: saying hello, finding the right description, and then checking back the description. Remember to take time to enjoy and savor these feelings.

At the question stage, positive feelings often appreciate slightly different questions. Try asking, "Is there something you want to show me or give me?" or "What do you need in order to be in my life more often?"

If you get both a positive and a negative feeling at the same time, you don't have to choose between them. Just be *in* the positive feeling, and from there, be *with* the not-so-positive feeling. For example, Bryan felt a warmth in his chest and a tightness in his stomach. He acknowledged both, then took some time to enjoy the warmth in his chest. He checked that "warmth" was the right word. He could sense that the warmth was connected to his love and enjoyment of his children. Then, staying in his chest, he turned his awareness also to the tightness in his stomach. He didn't go *into* the tightness in his stomach. He stayed *in* his chest, and *from there*, sensed his stomach. This was like letting the positive feeling (warmth) help him be a friend to the not-so-positive feeling (tightness). Bryan spent some time listening to what the tightness was about, from its point of view. He could use the warmth in his chest to help him find an attitude of friendliness and compassion for the tightness in his stomach. He discovered that his stomach was tightened with worry about whether his children would be all right. When he told his stomach that he heard its worry, it began to relax.

"I often see images when I close my eyes and feel in my body. Are images part of Focusing?"

Images certainly can be part of Focusing. If you take care to use your images wisely, they can advance your Focusing process. But there are some pitfalls to watch out for.

It is possible to get seduced by a fascinating series of images so that you forget about your body and just watch a sort of inner movie without feeling its connection to your body's felt sense.

When an image comes, notice if it is *in* your body, or if you seem to be seeing it in front of your eyes. This is the crucial question. Images *in* the body are called "body-felt images." Examples are: "I have a moss-covered rock in my stomach," or "There is a red rose in my heart." Images in front of the eyes are called "visual images." Examples are: "I see my mother's face," or "I see a lion pacing up and down in a cage."

If you have a body-felt image, an image in the body, there's no problem. Just treat it as you would any felt sense—say hello to it, sit with it, ask it questions if you want to. It's the visual image that might tempt you to get out of touch with your body. If you have a visual image, show it to your body, and ask your body how it feels about this image. Don't discard the image, but get a body feeling in addition to the image. If the image wants to change, ask again how the body feels. You can have as many images as you want, but don't forget to keep coming back to the body and checking how it feels.

Here is an example: Tony started Focusing by bringing awareness into his body and asking, "What wants to be known?" Instead of getting a body feeling, he got a visual image of a lion pacing up and down in a cage. So he asked himself, "As I see that image, how do I feel in my body?" He became aware of tightness in his chest. He stayed with the tightness *and* the image, and checked back with his body if the image of a lion pacing up and down in a cage fit the feeling of tightness. It did, and he then asked if there was a part of his life that was feeling this way. He realized that he was feeling this way at work. Continuing to be aware of the tightness in his chest, he empathized with how the lion was feeling. He became aware that the lion was feeling trapped and restless. He checked the words "trapped" and "restless" with the tightness in his chest, and they fit well. The session continued in this way, with Tony continuing to be aware of the image *and* body feeling, either of which might change in the process.

"What if I never get images? Can I still do Focusing?"

There seem to be people who get images easily, and others who don't. This has nothing to do with whether you can do Focusing. You can do Focusing successfully for the rest of your life and never get a single image. *If* images come, they can and should be included, but they are not required.

"What if I ask my felt sense what it needs, and it needs something I can't give it, or something I don't want to give it?"

Asking what your felt sense needs does not imply any promise that you can or will give it what it is asking for. Action needs to be clearly separated from any process of feeling and awareness. John is an example of a person who had not separated action from feeling. When I asked him if it would be OK to allow himself to feel his anger, he replied, "No, because if I feel my anger, I'll smash every window in this place." John had not yet discovered how to *feel* without *acting*.

When you ask your felt sense what it needs, your purpose should be to hear how it feels and to allow it to be fully understood. Whether or not it ever *gets* what it needs is another question, separate from *knowing* what it needs.

When you are Focusing, you are in touch with an ever-changing process. What feels right at this moment may evolve into something else in the next moment. That's why it doesn't make sense to get too involved in a particular step. If your inside place asks for something impossible, or illegal, or dangerous, don't say to it, "I can't do *that*!" You will stop your process. Don't even get into the issue of whether what it wants is going to happen. Instead, acknowledge that it wants that, and ask to hear more.

Let's say I'm Focusing on what's needed in my life, and I get a feeling that what would be *just right* would be to get on a plane *today* and fly to Tahiti. One possible response is to tell my body all the reasons why that isn't a good idea. But that won't help me move forward. So I'll just acknowledge that feeling, and listen to it, and invite it to say more. Maybe next I sense that what is so right about Tahiti is that I could completely relax, with no obligations. Then I ask my body for more about that. In a little while I find out that my present life really does feel full of obligations, and I hadn't been acknowledging that feeling. I then feel relief—and no more need to go to Tahiti. (But perhaps now my need is to give myself more personal relaxation time.)

So remember not to get into an argument with your body. You don't have to do what it says, and you don't have to say no either. If it wants something, just say, "I hear you," and keep listening.

Yet the other side of the coin is that *avoiding* action steps can be a block to Focusing. If your process tells you, over and over, that some course of action is right, and you don't actually get out there and *do* it, you won't ever move to the next step in your Focusing. This is because Focusing is not separate from life; it's part of life, and sometimes an action in your life is the next step that moves your Focusing process forward.

For example, you are Focusing on what to do to move your business forward, and what comes is that you could call up the local public access cable station and find out how to get on TV. But you don't do it. So the next time you sit down to focus on the same question, the same answer comes. Of course you can focus on what's in the way of making the call. But at some point, you have to take action for that part of your life to move forward.

The action doesn't have to be the big step that your inner Critic demands you take. It's better to ask your body for a step forward that feels *possible*, even if it's a small one. I heard a story of a man who focused on how lonely he was, and how hard it was to meet people. He asked his body what would be a positive step forward. The answer was, "It's too scary to actually attend a dance at the school, but I could call and find out when they are." So he did that. The next week he focused and his body said, "It's too scary to actually go into the dance, but I could go and peek in the door." So he did that. The next week he went in for one song . . . and so on. By the end of the semester he was meeting people and having a good time.

"When I'm Focusing, I start feeling bad about myself."

Your inner Critic is the harsh voice that attacks you with shaming accusations like "What makes you think you're any good?" "You'll fail at this just like you've failed at everything else!" "People will never like you if you don't quit being so selfish!" "What a stupid way to feel!" "You're so inarticulate!" And on and on. Take a moment to remember what your inner Critic sounds like and feels like. You have one; we all do.

Being under "Critic attack" can feel very bad. Your whole body may feel beaten up as you reel under the accusations of badness and wrongness that are coming at you from this unloving inner voice. A very big part of you believes this is true; you *are* bad, you *are* wrong. The first step to getting out from under is identifying what is happening. Try saying, "That's my Critic." Try saying hello to your inner Critic.

Once you have identified your inner Critic as a part of you rather than the Voice of Truth, you may be tempted to try to get rid of it. And you may well be able to push it away, for now. But the relief of pushing it away will be only temporary, because you haven't really resolved anything.

Think of the Critic as an unhealed part of you that has been cut off from love and acceptance. It speaks harshly because it has been unloved for so long. It needs to be integrated and included into your life, not cut off even more. But what needs to be integrated is what is *under* the critical voice, which is not criticism, but feeling.

The Critic is always afraid of something. After you have said hello to it, try asking it, gently and compassionately, "Is there something you're afraid of?" When it expresses its fears, just hear them. Don't try to respond, other than to say, "I hear you." Then ask, "And what are you wanting?" By doing this, you will receive the Critic's gifts, and release yourself from its attacks. (See the section on "Forming a better relationship with the inner Critic" in Chapter Seven.)

"What if I'm just making this up?"

The Doubter is the voice that tells you, during Focusing, that your experience isn't real, that you're making it up, or that nothing is happening. Sound familiar? Most people bump up against this questioning inner voice sometime in their Focusing, and those of us who try to rule our lives by logic tend to hear it even more. Focusing teacher Barbara McGavin calls the Doubter "the part of you that wants to make sure that all your experience is *real.*"

Making sure all your experience is real is a worthy cause. The problem is, the Doubter isn't raising this question in a way that's likely to be helpful. As far as the Doubter is concerned, if something *can* be doubted, then it doubts it! "But I *could* be making all this up out of my imagination. How do I know I'm not?"

The Doubter cannot resolve the doubts it raises. It doesn't have the tools. It doesn't know any way to confirm the realness of the experience that it's doubting; it only doubts. But Focusing *does* have a way to confirm your experience: coming back into your body, and checking there.

If the Doubter comes up at the beginning of the session and doubts whether you're getting a real felt sense, try saying to yourself, "Anything is something." Don't try to analyze or prejudge whether you've got the "right" felt sense or a "real" felt sense. Just be with whatever you *are* aware of, and follow it. You'll get somewhere—trust me!

The Doubter may come up in the middle of the session and doubt if what you're getting is "really" from the felt sense, or from your head or your imagination. Just check whatever you're getting back with your body and see if it feels right. Remember: it doesn't matter where it came from. What matters is, does it feel right?

The Doubter may even come at the end of your Focusing session. In one class a woman had a remarkable session, with shift after shift. After it was over she opened her eyes and said, "It's too bad this doesn't work for me." Everyone's jaw dropped! That was the Doubter at its worst. If you let it, it would be glad to wipe out whatever you receive from Focusing. Just remember: the Doubter does *not* tell the truth. It doubts whatever can be doubted. Come back to your body; that's where the truth is.

"When I ask the felt sense questions, my head answers."

When you ask a question of a felt sense in your body, your head (that is, your logical thinking capacity) may answer instead. Logical answers tend to come quickly rather than slowly, and they tend to be what you already know rather than something new or surprising.

If you get a quick answer to a question you're asking in your body, thank your head for the help and ask it to wait till later, and then ask the question in your body again.

But if a thought comes into your mind after you have been with the sense for a while, check with the sense to see if it fits. This may be the way your answer wanted to come to you, this time. You don't need to know *before* you check with your body if the right words came; that's what checking with your body is for. See the previous section on the inner Doubter.

"I get impatient with my Focusing process."

Impatience can result in rushing the inner process—and that is a block to Focusing. Be sure to notice if you are approaching your felt sense with a quality of impatience, annoyance, or hurry. If you are, acknowledge that. See if you can have both the feeling and the impatience about it—in different places. If necessary, you may want to focus on the impatience itself. One woman discovered a memory of her father saying, "If you won't tell me what you're crying about, I'll give you something to cry about!" She had taken that inside and was approaching any felt sense with the attitude of, "Tell me what you're about right now, or else!" Naturally this made Focusing more difficult. But after this realization, the impatient quality eased and she was able to allow her senses more time to be unknown and unclear.

"I'm afraid of what I might find out."

If you're afraid of what you find in your body, or of what you might find, there's a special move that's very helpful. Of course, just telling yourself not to be afraid probably won't help. But what you can do is turn toward your fear and focus on *that*. Bring your gentle, compassionate awareness to the part of you that's afraid; sit down with it and ask it to tell you more about how it feels.

There are two possible blocks here: to think you have to stop Focusing because there is fear *and* to think you have to push past the fear in order to get anywhere. Actually, by spending time with the fear you aren't missing anything; you are Focusing exactly where your body needs you to be.

Imagine you are standing with a child in front of a closed door. You want to open the door and go in; she is scared. You wouldn't force her to go, and you don't have to give up on going. Just kneel down beside her, put your arm around her, and say, "Please let me know what's so scary, honey." That's exactly the way to treat fear.

"What if I get two felt senses at once?"

It may well happen that you will get two felt senses at the same time (or even more than two), usually in different parts of your body. In this case it is important to respect and allow room for both, because both are important.

First, say hello to each one.

Next, ask this question in your body, "Does it feel right to stay with both for a while, or is one of them calling me more right now?" Even if one of the senses is calling you to be with it first, you will probably eventually spend time with the other one as well, and it's good to acknowledge that.

"I lose concentration; it's hard to stay with the process."

Losing concentration while Focusing is one of the most common difficulties reported to me. Your mind wanders, you "space out," you forget what you were doing, you daydream, you start thinking about your day ahead . . . and then you catch yourself and your inner Critic comes in, "This is hopeless! I can never do this Focusing! I might as well give up!"

I will show you a number of techniques for keeping your concentration while Focusing. Most of them involve being active in some way. The classic Focusing posture is similar to meditation: sitting up, eyes closed, attention silently inward. But there are more active ways to do Focusing, and you may find one of the other ways to be easier for you than the "classic" one.

Speaking

You can speak out loud while you are Focusing and listen to yourself. You'll hear yourself through another channel—your ears—and be able to check back your words more easily. The very act of putting your experience into words you say out loud will help you hold concentration. Have you ever had to count a large number of objects? Perhaps you noticed that if you counted out loud, you were better able to remember where you were in the counting. The principle here is the same. Say things like, "I'm feeling tightness in my chest right now." Then notice if what you said feels right, and continue from there.

You can also speak into a tape recorder. This gives you something to talk to, whether or not you ever play it back. If you do play it back, you might notice how your body feels as you do so.

Writing

Focusing combines well with another helpful method of self-exploration: keeping a journal. To use Focusing in combination with writing, have a piece of paper or a Focusing journal in front of you as you focus. Write down key words like the description, the questions you're asking, and whatever else feels important. If you lose your concentration, just open your eyes and read the last thing you've written.

Having a continuous record of your Focusing sessions can help you see the progress you're making and remember key insights that were important. Even if you don't write during the session, you may want to write in your Focusing journal afterward, so you have a record of your inner work.

Some people are comfortable with writing continuously while Focusing, in handwriting or at the computer. It might go something like this: "How am I in my body right now? I had a hard day today and my chest is feeling very tight about it. Let me see, is it tight? No, it's more like there's a pressure inside. That makes me think of all the things I'm feeling pressure about in my work. That report is overdue but I can't get into it; I'm just not convinced it's important. Is that what the pressure in my chest is about? No, that doesn't fit; it's something else . . ."

Drawing or painting

Especially if your felt senses have a visual quality, try drawing what you see and feel in your body. Use a medium you are comfortable with: watercolors, crayons, pastels, pencil, pen . . . You might even want to sculpt in clay the shape you are feeling inside.

As you draw, compare the drawing to the feeling, noticing if it feels right. Go ahead and change the drawing as necessary, to fit the feeling. After a session, some people draw images or symbols that were important during the session and record them in a Focusing journal.

Taking a walk

You don't have to sit still to Focus. You can take a walk, or do the dishes, or perform any routine task that doesn't take much attention. I like this way of Focusing, myself. If I lose concentration, I don't let loose the inner Critic on myself, because I'm not "supposed" to be Focusing. I'm simply taking a walk, and any Focusing that I do is extra! I can stop to admire a beautiful flower, or look both ways at an intersection, and then come back to the felt sense that I was spending time with. I find that the physical activity can actually refresh and enhance my Focusing.

Focusing with a friend

By far the ideal way to hold concentration is to focus with a friend—and that's what the next chapter is about.

Chapter Nine

Focusing with a Friend

You are now well on your way to doing Focusing whenever you need to. You do not need another person's help in order to focus. However, like many activities in life, Focusing is even more fun when you do it with a friend, and often more productive as well. The remaining three chapters of this book are about how to do Focusing with another person. In this chapter we learn how to focus with a friend. In the next chapter we see how to bring Focusing into your practice if you are a psychotherapist and, in the final chapter, how to bring Focusing into your therapy if you are a client.

Focusing partnerships

When you and a friend agree to practice Focusing together, you are forming a Focusing partnership, a relationship of equal exchange. It isn't like therapy, where one person gets paid and the other person gets the attention. In a Focusing partnership, you and your friend will divide the time equally and take turns in two roles.

The two roles are the "Focuser" and the "listener," the companion of the Focuser. When you get together for your Focusing partnership, one partner is the listener and the other is the Focuser. Then, in the second part of your Focusing time, you switch roles.

The main difference from Focusing alone will be that you, as the Focuser, are going to speak out loud, describing at least some of the things you are feeling and at least some of the steps you are going through. You will probably find that speaking out loud helps you to concentrate on your Focusing and to not drift away. But if you ever feel that speaking is going to interrupt your Focusing instead of helping it, don't speak. Your responsibility is to your Focusing process, not to entertaining the listener.

Now let's talk about what the listener does.

Being present

Being the listener involves, first of all, being present as yourself. Sit comfortably across from your friend and let go of having any agenda for this person. You don't need them to change; you don't need them to have a "good" session. Your job is just to be there. One way we say this in my classes is "holding the space." Your job is to hold the space.

As the listener, it's good to take some time to bring awareness into *your* body. Feel the contact of your body with the chair, be aware of the middle area of your body, throat, chest, stomach, and abdomen. If you have felt senses right now, say hello to them. Let them know their turn will come a little later.

Now turn your attention to your friend, the Focuser. In a moment she will begin to speak, and then you will begin to say back what you hear. Invite into yourself an attitude of appreciation for the jewel that this person is. Let your consciousness be like a quiet pool of water that is waiting to reflect the realness of your friend's process.

You are not the expert!

As a companion to another person's Focusing process, the hardest thing to remember—and the most important—is that you are not the expert. You are not the healer. You are not the fixer of this person's life.

If you're like most of us, this will be a rather new sensation. We're used to listening to our friends' problems and then offering suggestions. We're supposed to be "helpful." We feel we ought to get involved and shoulder a part of our friend's burden.

And there are times when this is appropriate. For example, my friend might be telling me his difficulties finding a good dentist, and I happen to know an excellent one.

But in helping someone else do Focusing, the attitude of "fixer" simply doesn't help at all. You'll get in the way of the process, and you'll wear yourself out, too. It's much more relaxing, and actually much more helpful, to sit back and remember that the person who's Focusing is the one responsible for the session—and for his life. You are the companion. Your job is to be present.

Practical listening

As the companion to a person who is Focusing, your first job is to be present. Your second job is to listen.

You may find that listening is hard—and new. How often do we *just* listen, without also thinking, analyzing, judging, or planning what we're going to say in response? You may discover that you're out of practice as a listener. If so, you'll almost certainly find that listening will be very rewarding to you. Among other things, it clears your mind of clutter!

But I hope I can convince you that listening is also easy. It's simple, it's restful, it's very much in present time. Listening to another person who is Focusing is one of the most meditative things that I do.

Practical listening is listening in such a way that your partner *knows* you are listening, and *can use* your listening to further her Focusing process. This simply means *saying back* or *reflecting* some of what your Focusing partner is saying. When your partner says, "I feel sad," you say, "You're sad." When your partner says, "I feel a tightness in my throat," you say, "You have a tightness, there in your throat." You are reflecting the words and feelings that your Focusing partner needs to hear.

Probably this will feel a bit strange at first. You may fear that you are sounding like a parrot, or a tape recorder. But just wait until you switch places with your partner, and it's your turn to focus. Wait until you find out how wonderful it feels to have someone say back your words, and nothing more, so you have the luxury to explore your feelings further. That's when you'll know a good listener is worth her weight in gold!

The Focuser listens to the listener

The key to great listening has nothing to do with the expertise of the listener. The key to great listening is that the Focuser *listens* to the listener, and checks those words inside to make sure they are right. When you are Focusing, you can use the listener to the fullest by taking the listener's words down into your body, down to the place where your words first came from. If you feel tightness in your throat, and the listener says back "tightness in your throat," don't just be polite and say, "Yes, that's what I said." This is no place for politeness! Really check—take the word "tightness" back into your throat, and see if that word really fits. Maybe it does. Great! That will help you stay with the feeling and listen for more. But maybe "tightness" is actually not quite right. Maybe it's really "squeezing," or "constriction," or "desperate." Hearing your own words back in the listener's voice will help you get closer to what is really true for you.

What to listen for

When you are the listener, you don't want to say back everything your partner said. For one thing, that would be very difficult, especially if he said a lot! (Remember, I said listening doesn't need to be difficult. So if you're finding it difficult, you're probably working harder than you need to!)

If you don't say back everything, you'll need to choose what to listen for and what to say back. Here are some tips on what to listen for.

Feelings and emotions. Say back your partner's feelings and emotions. Feelings can include body words like "tight," "heavy," or "jumpy," and emotion words like "scared," "mad," or "joyful." Say back the words by themselves, or even better put them in short sentences like, "You feel scared," or "That place feels tight."

Focuser: I'm scared because I don't know whether I'm going to be able to finish this project, and there's a lot riding on it.

Listener: You're feeling scared right now.

Present time. Say back what your partner is feeling or sensing *right now*, as opposed to what he felt yesterday or last week.

Focuser: I'm feeling tight across my chest, and it's the same place that was feeling so relaxed yesterday.

Listener: You're feeling tight across your chest.

The last thing. If your partner says a lot before pausing to let you reflect, don't worry, and don't try to remember it all. It's almost always most helpful just to say back the last thing he said.

Focuser: I really don't know what this heaviness in my heart is all about. It reminds me of a way that I felt one year in college. I had just broken up with my first boyfriend, and I was convinced that I would be lonely the rest of my life. Oh! I see! It has to do with my friend Paula moving away. There's something in me that thinks I'll never find a friend as close as Paula.

Listener: There's something in you that thinks you'll never find a friend as close as Paula.

Anything you hear twice. If the Focuser repeats something, that's your signal that he really wants to hear that back from you. Say back anything you hear twice, even if it's something that *isn't* emotions, or present time, or the last thing.

Focuser: I'm scared because I don't know whether I'm going to be able to finish this project, and there's a lot riding on it.

Listener: You're feeling scared.

Focuser: Because there's a lot riding on it.

Listener: Because there's a *lot* riding on it!

Advanced listening

When you do what I call advanced listening, you are permitted to change or add to your Focusing partner's words, just a little, in order to facilitate the accepting attitude of Focusing.

"Part of you feels . . ." Whenever your partner says, "I am . . ." or "I feel . . ." you are allowed to say back "Part of you is . . ." or "Part of you feels. . . ." This is a simple but enormously helpful move that will enable your partner to experience her separateness from her feelings, so she won't be so easily overwhelmed by them.

Focuser: I am very sad about all this loss in my life.

Listener: Part of you is very sad about all this loss in your life.

and:

Focuser: I feel crazy when there are five million things going
on at once.

Listener: Part of you feels crazy when there are five million
things going on at once.

"Something." The word "something" is worth its weight in
gold to a listener, and to a Focuser, too. It enables the listener to be a
companion to a body awareness that cannot yet be described. It helps
the Focuser bring awareness to what she *does* feel, rather than concentrating on what she doesn't know.

Focuser: I don't know what to call this feeling in my throat.

Listener: You're feeling *something* in your throat.

Remember: "I don't know" is in the head. "I feel something" is
in the body. Whenever you hear your Focuser say "I don't know," see
if you can reflect "you feel something." Another example:

Focuser: I don't know what this part of me is scared of.

Listener: This part of you is scared of *something*.

Putting a gentle emphasis on the word "something" helps to
indicate that it's pointing to a real experience, not just holding an
empty place in the sentence. You are in essence inviting the Focuser to
feel into the *something* that is there.

Guiding

Sometimes your partner's Focusing process needs something more
than listening. Then you can do some guiding. Guiding is making
suggestions like "Maybe you could notice how you're feeling in your
body right now." Suggestions can help support your partner's Focusing. Remember: you can make suggestions about the Focusing process, but not about your partner's life!

The other thing to remember is that even if you're guiding, you
still are not the expert, or the healer, or the fixer. You are still there as
the *companion* for your partner's Focusing process. And your partner
is still the ultimate judge of what is helpful. So if you offer a guiding
suggestion, always be willing for your partner to say, "Actually, I

don't want to do that right now." And be glad that he is in touch with what he wants!

Probably the easiest way to guide is to hold in your hand a version of the Focusing phrases that we learned in Chapters Four and Five, rephrased as suggestions to another person instead of to one's self. But please *don't* simply read these in order! If you feel that a suggestion is needed rather than just listening, use your intuition to choose the one suggestion that might be appropriate, and then go back to listening for a while.

Guiding Phrases

- "Take some time to sense into your body."

- "You might ask in there, 'What wants my awareness now?' (or 'How am I about that issue?')"

- "Take some time to say hello to that."

- "You might notice what's the best way to describe that."

- "Notice if it's OK to just be with this right now."

- "You might sit with it, with interested curiosity."

- "Take some time to sense how *it* feels, from *its* point of view."

- "You might ask if it has an emotional quality."

- "You might ask it, 'What gets it so _____?'" Fill in the appropriate emotion or description word.

- "You might ask it what it needs."

- "You might ask your body to show you how 'all OK' would feel."

- "See if you'd like to check if it's OK to stop soon."

- "You might tell it that you'll be back."

- "Take some time to thank your body and the parts that have been with you."

Now I'll say more about some of the specific guiding suggestions.

"Take some time to say hello to that."

The single most helpful phrase in guiding is this one: "Take some time to say hello to that." If you add only one guiding suggestion to your partnership, let it be this one. Another way to say it is, "See if it's OK to say hello to that." "That" refers to a felt sense or feeling of some kind.

> *Focuser:*   I'm feeling a tight place in my chest, connected with the presentation tomorrow.
>
> *Listener:*   There's a tight place in your chest.
>
> *Focuser:*   It feels scared.
>
> *Listener:*   A scared feeling. See if it's OK to say hello to that.

What's wonderful about this suggestion is that it reminds you and your partner that *being* is the essence of Focusing. If you're tempted to solve the problem or be helpful, or if your partner is tempted to make an effort to fix things up in the inner world, "See if it's OK to say hello to that" is a reminder to let go of fixing and solving and simply come into contact with the feeling, just as it is right now.

> *Focuser:*   "There's a big, anxious feeling about my work."
>
> *Listener:*   "You're sensing a big, anxious feeling there, about your work."
>
> *Focuser:*   "I'm trying to think what I can do to make it feel better."
>
> *Listener:*   "See if it's OK to just say hello to that anxious feeling."

Coming back to the body

It's easy to lose contact with body awareness at various points during the Focusing process, and it's great to have a listening partner who can remind you to bring awareness back to your body when you need that.

When would you do this? One good time is when your partner says she feels lost. (In these examples we're assuming that the Focuser feels lost in relation to the Focusing process itself. The listener would respond differently if the Focuser says she's lost in relation to her life or a life issue.)

Focuser: I don't know where I am now.

Listener: Maybe you could just sense how you are in your body.

or:

Focuser: I feel lost.

Listener: You might just notice how your body is feeling now.

There are three other good times to remind your Focusing partner to sense in her body. People can sometimes get drawn away from body awareness by thoughts, images, and even emotions.

Thoughts

Focuser: I have this angry feeling in my gut.

Listener: You're aware of an angry feeling.

Focuser: I'm thinking it really isn't important; there's no reason to be angry.

Listener: And maybe you could just notice how your body is feeling right now.

Images

Focuser: I see a flowing pattern of light. It's wide at the top and bottom and narrow in the middle. There are sparkles all through it.

Listener: There's a flowing pattern of light with sparkles. Notice if this is the right time to sense how all that is feeling in your body.

Emotions

Focuser: I'm very sad today.

Listener: See if it's OK to sense where in your body you're feeling so sad.

The feeling about the feeling

If the Focuser is not able to hold an inner attitude of friendship and acceptance, he needs to move his awareness to the part that can't be accepting. Whenever the Focuser has a feeling of not accepting or not liking what's there, then *that* is what should receive his accepting attention.

> *Focuser:*   I'd like to push this away.
>
> *Listener:*   Maybe you could just say hello to that feeling of wanting to push this away.
>
> or:
>
> *Focuser:*   I'm angry with this sad feeling.
>
> *Listener:*   See if it's OK to just be with the anger.

Suggesting helpful questions

If your Focusing partner asks you for help in thinking of a good question to ask her felt sense, don't panic. *Any* question you suggest will be helpful. If the question you suggest isn't the right question for this person at this moment, hearing it will probably help her sense what *is* the right question.

Remember, asking questions of the felt sense comes *after* describing the felt sense, checking back the description, and seeing if it's OK to just be with it. The most common reason for getting nothing in answer to an inner question is that it was asked too soon.

Here are three of the most helpful questions to ask the felt sense:

- "You might notice if this has some emotional quality." (If you haven't heard an emotion word yet.)

- "You might ask it what gets it so _____." Fill in the blank with the emotion word that the Focuser has already used.

- "You might ask it what it needs from you right now."

Whenever possible, use the Focuser's key words in the questions you suggest.

> *Focuser:*   It's very sad.
>
> *Listener:*   You might want to ask it, "What gets it so sad?"

or:

Focuser:	Something is pressing on me in here.
Listener:	Notice if you'd like to ask it, "What's so important to it about pressing on you?"

or:

Focuser:	Part of me is angry about the situation at work.
Listener:	See if it would be right to ask it, "What is it about the situation at work that gets it the angriest?"

Notice that the listener does not ask questions. The listener *suggests* that the Focuser ask the question. The listener's questions will bring the Focuser out of herself. Suggestions and listening responses will help her stay in her inner process.

Chapter Ten

Especially for Therapists

If you're a therapist reading this book, you've probably already been thinking about how an awareness of the Focusing process can enhance your work with your clients. You don't have to become a "Focusing therapist" in order to bring in Focusing as another aspect of your practice. You've probably studied a number of different techniques and methods already and use whatever is appropriate to each client's needs. Awareness of the Focusing process can be another one of your tools.

"Easy" clients and "tough" clients

As a therapist, you have some clients whose sessions are always a treat to look forward to. No matter how tough their life is, they always get some movement and clarity in the session. Both of you feel good when the session is over, satisfied and pleased with the progress made.

Then you have other clients who seem stuck, both to themselves and to you. You don't see movement and change, either in their sessions or their lives. They ask you, "Shouldn't something more be happening?" and you reassure them, and yourself, that sometimes change is slow, and patience is necessary. But those are not the clients you look forward to. When you get a cancellation from this type of client, some part of you feels relief.

It is quite true that sometimes change is slow, and patience is necessary. But often the painfully slow process of these "tough" clients comes from the fact that they are out of touch with the source of change. They are either in their heads, intellectualizing and analyzing, or they are caught up in a cycle of repetitive emotion.

Thoughts and emotions can accompany change, but they are not the source of change. The source of change is the body as sensed in the present moment. By the use of subtle and non-intrusive interventions, you can help your clients come into contact with the felt sense level of experiencing in their bodies. You may not turn all your "tough" clients into "easy" ones, but you and your clients will more often feel that satisfying sense that "something" is happening, however slowly.

"And how did *you* feel about that?"

A key prerequisite for Focusing is that your clients be in touch with their own perspectives, their own points of view, and their own reactions to the events they are dealing with. If your client is talking about what other people did and felt, and narrating events from an external perspective without mentioning her own feelings and reactions, it will be difficult for her to get to Focusing from there. Inviting her to feel in her body at that point will probably be confusing.

As a bridge, first help your clients become aware of their own perspective. After a story about what other people did, you might ask, "And how was that for you?" or "What was your reaction to that?" or "How did you feel when that happened?"

This may take patience. As I'm sure you've already observed, when feelings are unfamiliar territory, they don't come easily just because they've been invited with one question. In answer to your question, "And how was that for you?" your client may reply, "Well, it was just too late. There was nothing anyone could do." She is simply not aware that she has not yet expressed her own feelings. You will need to gently persist: "Yes, it was too late. And you felt—how?"

Clients who are unfamiliar with the vocabulary of feeling may need this process modeled; for example, you may need to guess at their feelings, and make sure there is room for them to amend your guess. "I'm imagining that you might have felt really sad about that. Would 'sad' be right?"

"And how is that for you right now?"

Another prerequisite, after being able to access and express feelings, is being able to access and express *present* feelings.

> *Client:* I've been walking around feeling disappointed all week.
>
> *Therapist:* M-hm. Disappointed.
>
> *Client:* I like telling people I'm disappointed better than telling them I'm depressed. My son has a much easier time with the word "disappointed."
>
> *Therapist:* I wonder if you are feeling disappointed or depressed right now?

In this excerpt, the client begins by expressing a feeling from his own perspective, and it isn't clear whether he is feeling it in the present, although he might be. However, he then goes on to talk about his son's reaction to the words he uses, rather than pursuing the feeling of disappointment in the present. So the therapist intervenes, inviting his awareness to what is presently felt.

Like being able to feel from his own perspective, being aware of present feelings might require practice on the client's part, and patience on yours.

Bringing in the body

After your client is experiencing feelings in the present time, it's an easy and natural step to invite her to notice how her body holds those feelings.

> *Therapist:* I wonder if you are feeling disappointed right now?
>
> *Client:* Yes, I am, actually.
>
> *Therapist:* And can you sense maybe where in your body you're feeling that disappointed?
>
> *Client:* Well . . . it's mostly in my heart.

What's next? See the section on "Guiding" in the previous chapter for some of the suggestions we've used to help a person stay with a felt sense in Focusing. Of course you would adapt them to the needs of your circumstances. I've been told by one therapist, for example, that although suggesting that someone say hello to a feeling sounds fine in the context of a Focusing workshop, it sounds odd as a suggestion in a therapy session. (Try instead "You might want to acknowledge that.")

Here is a possible continuation of the session about the disappointed feeling that shows some of the Focusing suggestions you might use.

Therapist: Ah, yes, you're sensing it in your heart. You might just check if the word "disappointed" is still the best word for how it's feeling in your heart right now.

Client: (pause, eyes closed) Right now I'm feeling it's very sad right there.

Therapist: You might see if it's OK to just stay with that feeling of sad in your heart.

Client: (slow tears leak out) It feels good to stay with it.

Therapist: (after a respectful silence) You might ask that feeling of sad if there's something it wants you to know.

Client: It says . . . This sounds funny, but it says it wants me to slow down and listen to my own heartbeat!

Therapist: Ah!

Client: (more tears) I've been listening so much to other people's voices.

Therapist: The sad place in your heart says it wants you to slow down and listen to your own heartbeat.

Client: Yes . . . Except it isn't sad any more.

Therapist: How is it feeling now?

Client: It feels . . . There's a lightness in there now. A feeling of hopefulness. There's hope.

Listening

I'm sure you noticed in the excerpt above that sometimes the therapist repeats the client's words. Listening, or active listening, or reflection of feeling, or empathic reflection, is taught in many counseling courses and is an important aspect of many modes of therapy. Done well, it can be enormously facilitative. Done badly, it can make the therapist sound mechanical, distant, and unskilled. Naturally, we are only recommending that it be done well!

We've seen that Focusing involves "staying with" an inner awareness. A listening reflection can help the client stay with the feeling or sensation that is expressed in the reflected words. See "Practical listening" in the preceding chapter. Choosing to reflect present feelings can help the client stay with and explore them, instead of moving into self-analysis or self-criticism.

Listening for the "edge" of experience

In Chapter One I described the research that led to the description of Focusing. It was observed that at some point in a session, successful therapy clients would *slow down* their talk, become *less articulate*, and begin to *grope for words* to describe something they were feeling at that moment. You can become a highly effective facilitator of your clients' change process if you listen for and encourage these moments, which Gendlin refers to as the "edge" of experience.

Your client probably does not yet understand that these moments of groping to describe something presently felt are so valuable. He may hurry past them, eager to get to something more clear and explicable. You can help him value and stay with these rich sources of inner depth.

For example, imagine a client saying something like this: "I think it must be a kind of denial. I'm feeling . . . it's hard to describe . . . kind of a wall inside. No, that's not quite it. It's . . . it's . . . I don't know. It's just very vague right now. I guess I'm being resistant."

How might you respond to this segment? Notice the two sentences at the beginning and the end: "I think it must be a kind of denial," and "I guess I'm being resistant." The words "think" and "guess" as well as the pop psych jargon ("denial" and "resistant") are clues that these sentences are straight out of the client's head. But the middle of the segment—"I'm feeling . . . it's hard to describe . . . kind of a wall inside. No, that's not quite it. It's . . . it's . . . I don't know. It's just very vague right now."—seems to indicate direct contact with a felt sense. As we've seen, felt senses are hard to stay with. It takes a lot of faith to value something so vague. This is the place where the therapist can help, enormously. Any of the following responses would encourage the Focusing aspect of this client's process: "Kind of a wall inside, but that's not quite it," "You're feeling something vague," "It feels like something stops you, maybe, or cuts you off," or "You might just stay with that feeling that's hard to describe."

Notice that the first three responses are all types of listening, or reflection, and the fourth is a gentle suggestion just to stay with something. When you choose to reflect the "edge" of experience, your client is encouraged to stay with it. On the other hand, this response would *not* facilitate Focusing in this client: "You think this is a kind of denial." Choosing to reflect a mental, analytical statement does not take a client more deeply into a Focusing process.

Appreciating your client's No

As you make listening reflections, and guiding suggestions, be sure to be open to the possibility that what you are offering won't be quite right for your client, won't "fit." Focusing teaches us that it is more important for the client to be in a process of inner sensing, and checking with her own felt sense, than for the therapist to be right!

By virtue of your role, your words tend to be given more weight by your client than the suggestions of a friend, say. To counterbalance this tendency, you might offer occasional suggestions that the client might check your words, as well as her own, with her actual body sense.

> *Client:*   I'm feeling really, sort of . . . trapped, I guess.
>
> *Therapist:* It sounds like you might be feeling very helpless.
>
> *Client:*   I guess so.
>
> *Therapist:* You might just check with your body, to see if helpless is right, or maybe trapped fits better.
>
> *Client:*   No, it's neither one . . . Uh . . . It's more like . . .

Listen especially for the times when your client wants to tell you, "No, that's not quite right." Obviously it would miss the point to interpret this as resistance or as a transference issue with you. This "no" is not about you, certainly not in a negative way. It's a sign that your client is in touch with something that is more than words can capture easily, and trusts you enough to take the time to sense that more deeply. If you can welcome and appreciate your client's no, you'll be encouraging the fine differentiation of experience that moves the Focusing process forward.

When your client doesn't feel enough

Movement and change in therapy can be difficult when your client is out of touch with his own feelings. Focusing offers ways to help facilitate more awareness of feelings. You'll recognize that you're dealing with a person who needs this kind of help when you try a few of the suggestions already discussed, and you're met with blankness.

> *Client:* They really gave me the runaround.
>
> *Therapist:* And how did you feel when that happened?
>
> *Client:* I felt that they should be prosecuted.
>
> *Therapist:* And how are you feeling right now?
>
> *Client:* I don't know.

This is probably not so much a matter of resistance as it is a matter of unfamiliarity with the process of feeling itself. Part of your job, then, is to facilitate feeling ability. One technique for this is to guide your client through a guided exercise in feeling (see "Attunement" later in this chapter). If you have guided your client into body awareness, and he still feels "nothing," there are two techniques which are very likely to be helpful: feeling difference, and feeling something positive.

Feeling difference

The easiest thing to feel is a *difference*, because the client doesn't have to know *what* he's feeling, just that it feels different from something else he's feeling.

> *Client:* (after being led through the attunement) It just feels blank all through my throat and chest and stomach.
>
> *Therapist:* OK. So you might take some time just to notice your throat. And then notice if the way it feels blank in

> your throat feels *different* from the way it feels blank
> in your chest.

Client: They feel about the same.

Therapist: Uh-huh. And now notice your chest. And then notice
             if the way it feels blank in your chest feels different
             from the way it feels blank in your stomach.

Client: Well, my stomach is actually a little tight . . .

Feeling something positive

Interestingly, when we are asked to notice how we feel, we often
tend to ignore positive feelings. It's understandable, given the context
of therapy, that when a client is asked to look for a feeling, he looks
for something negative or unpleasant. But when the *process of feeling*
needs practice, it is just as important to be aware of feelings experienced as pleasant or positive.

Client: (after being led through the attunement) I don't feel
             anything in there, that I'm aware of.

Therapist: And you might notice if perhaps you're feeling
             something positive in there, like open or relaxed or
             peaceful.

Client: Well, actually, I am feeling very open in my chest.

Therapist: So you might take some time to be with that open
             feeling in your chest.

Client: Yes, that feels good . . . And now I'm noticing that my
             stomach is a little tight . . .

When your client feels too much

Of course strong emotion and cathartic process are welcome in a therapy office, as the ubiquitous box of tissues attests. But there are times
when your client may be experiencing strong or intense emotions in
such a way that forward movement is blocked. Sometimes this is
because the client becomes frightened of the intensity of the feeling,
and stops it. Other times the intensity of the feeling interferes with the
client's ability to sense fine distinctions, just as music played too loud
prevents hearing the details of the melody.

The key that Focusing offers is dis-identification. This is the difference between "I am sad" and "A part of me is sad." Dis-identification gives the client the ability to experience the feeling just as *strongly*, but from a slightly different perspective. The client becomes the observer or the witness to the feeling, without at all muting or denying its intensity.

There are a number of techniques that help with dis-identification. Inviting a client to notice *where in the body* she is feeling some emotion is actually a dis-identification technique, because her awareness becomes more localized.

Listen for the times when you hear, "I am . . ." as in "I am sad," "I am angry," "I am scared." Invite the client to try out, "Part of me is . . ." or "Part of me feels . . ." instead.

Client: I'm starting to get overwhelmed. I'm just so terrified!

Therapist: Can we say there's a *part* of you that's so terrified?

Client: It's a big part.

Therapist: Yes, it's really a big part.

Client: OK. (takes a big breath) I can say that. It's terrified of . . .

Notice that this client goes on to sense more about "terrified" after she is able to get a slight perspective on it through dis-identification, and this is quite typical.

See "Being in a relationship with your feelings" and "Being a friend to your felt sense" in Chapter Three.

Starting the session

Attunement

You may want to use a Focusing "attunement" at the start of a session, especially when the client has said, "I have no idea what I want to work on." You can suggest the possibility of using a process to get in touch with something, and when the client agrees, say something like this:

"So you might just take some time to get comfortable in your chair . . . . And just begin letting your awareness come into your body, maybe first being aware of your hands . . . and your feet . . . being aware of the contact of your body on the chair. . . . Now let your awareness come inward, into the whole inner area of your body that includes your throat, your chest, your stomach and abdomen. And just let your awareness rest gently in that whole middle area. And maybe give yourself a gentle invitation in there, like you're saying, 'What's here now?' or 'What wants my awareness now?' And then wait, and when you become aware of *something*, you might let me know."

Speak slowly, and allow pauses. The pace and tone of your words will facilitate your client's process. You may even want to follow along in your own body. As you say "Maybe first being aware of your hands," be aware of your own hands, and so on. This will give a natural timing to your words and help to include your own inner awareness in the therapy process. See the section on "The therapist's felt senses" later in this chapter.

Clearing a space

You can also use a Focusing process called "clearing a space" when a client says, "I don't have anything to talk about this week." Clearing a space is a way of taking inventory of what is going on.

Begin in the same way as in the attunement given above. Then, after inviting awareness to the whole middle area, ask, "What's in the way of feeling really wonderful about how your life is going?"

As the client identifies each thing, the therapist invites him to acknowledge it in some way, and then set it down for now, like setting down something that one is carrying. When the client nods or gives a sign that this one is set down, the therapist says, "So now, what else is in the way of feeling really wonderful about your life?" If the client has difficulty in setting something down, imagery may be helpful, such as, "You might imagine you are setting each thing on a table or shelf beside you."

In this process, the client may naturally move into beginning to work with something, and that of course is fine. But if he completes the process of setting down everything that comes up and says something like, "That's all," then the therapist can ask him to choose one of those things to work with. One way to invite this is to say, "Imagine that there is a magnet in the middle of your body so you can feel which one is drawing you the most right now."

See also "I can't focus on one thing; there are too many things going on," in Chapter Eight.

Facilitating the attitude of gentleness

One of the gifts of Focusing is that it lets your client have a more gentle and accepting relationship with herself. It can be excruciating to hear a client reject her own inner experience, the more so when we know that this harshness to the self will delay the process of change: "This is a stupid way to feel," or "I wish my anger would just go away," or "I'm such an inarticulate person."

The first step to gentleness is dis-identification: "So there's a part of you that feels that this is a stupid way to feel," or "So there's a part of you that wants your anger to just go away," or "So there's a part of you that feels you're an inarticulate person, and doesn't like that." This process alone will probably bring something of a shift for the client.

Then you can invite your client's acceptance of the feeling she was rejecting by using language that feels appropriate in your setting, like: "So you might see if, just for now, you could allow your anger to be there, with the idea that it *will* change, after you have heard its message."

If the rejection persists, however, then that becomes the object of attention.

> *Client:*   I wish my anger would just go away.
>
> *Therapist:* So there's a part of you that wants your anger to just go away. And you might see if, just for now, you could allow your anger to be there, with the idea that it *will* change, after you have heard its message.
>
> *Client:*   I can't. I don't want to be angry.
>
> *Therapist:* OK. So maybe just acknowledge the part of you that doesn't want to be angry, and see if there's more about that.
>
> *Client:*   It feels like . . . it feels like if people see I'm angry then they can hurt me.

There might be other moments when, even without the appearance of harshness, you get the intuition that inner gentleness would be a welcome addition to the process. These are often times when something comes in the client that is felt as tender, vulnerable, or raw in some way.

> *Client:* I'm feeling something right here (points to chest) that feels very shy.
>
> *Therapist:* (in a gentle tone of voice) Yes. Something is there, and it feels very shy.
>
> *Client:* (tears) It's feeling very tender and vulnerable right now.
>
> *Therapist:* And maybe you could be gentle to that tender and vulnerable place, and just let it know that you're with it.

Facilitating the inner relationship

The suggestion "And maybe you could be gentle to that tender and vulnerable place, and just let it know that you're with it," is an example of a very powerful kind of work using Focusing, which is called "facilitating the inner relationship."

This helps your client develop a positive and nurturing relationship with his inner self. So you give gentle suggestions to facilitate that relationship, such as, "You might let that part of you know that you hear it."

Those familiar with inner child work will see the similarity. The difference is that there is no need to personify the felt sense as a child. If it feels like a child to the client, that is welcome, but if not, it can still be given gentleness, acceptance, and listening. For many people this is easier to do than to first experience an inner child and then give it loving attention. So you will find people who have difficulty working with an inner child but have no difficulty developing a nurturing relationship with a shy, sad, or vulnerable felt sense.

Facilitating action steps

The process of inner awareness is incomplete if it does not also lead to a new way of behaving and living. At the early stages of change it is important just to feel how things are. Later, your client will be ready to take her new awareness into action in her life. She will tell you when she reaches this stage.

> *Client:* I feel like I'm just rehashing the same things over and over but I'm not making any changes.

Therapist: It sounds as if you're feeling it's time to take some action. Is that right?

Client: Yes, exactly.

Therapist: How about if you tell me what your intentions are, what you would like to see.

Client: I would like to really open up to my husband more, on an ongoing basis.

Therapist: Is that an intention?

Client: Well, yes, I know I have to do it.

Therapist: So it's really a commitment, then?

Client: Yes.

Therapist: So you might take some time to notice how that feels in your body, if you make that commitment, to open up to your husband more on an ongoing basis. Notice how it feels in your body to move forward now with that commitment.

Client: It feels good. Very solid, especially in my arms.

Therapist: So let yourself just feel that good, solid feeling. And let your imagination go forward to the week to come, and notice what specific steps come from this commitment and this feeling.

Focusing and therapy are not separate from life. Human lives are an interplay between feeling and action. Our clients may need to live for a while with a new way of being, and with the action that emerges from it, before further processing can occur. As Helene Brenner says, "Sometimes the answers come through action. Some results don't come about just through process."

Beginning to work in a new way

The suggestions offered here may be totally consistent with the way you already work with your clients, or they may represent somewhat of a shift in attitude and language. If you have been working with someone for a long time, you may want to introduce a changed way of working by saying something like, "Today let's try something different and see how it feels. During today's session, I'm going to be inviting you to pay more attention to how your body is feeling. Don't worry, there isn't any way to do this wrong."

In most cases, however, there will be no need to introduce the changes you are making, because they can be integrated into the way you are already working. Your part of a session with Focusing awareness will sound almost the same as always, with perhaps a few sentences added. It is the client's part of the session that may differ dramatically.

The therapist's felt senses

Bringing Focusing into your practice of psychotherapy isn't only about your client's felt senses. It's also about your own. Staying present in your body during your sessions can be beneficial in a number of ways.

Enhancing your intuition. As you listen to your client and stay present in your body, you may be aware of feelings or images that are not from your logical mind. There may be a time when it feels right to share them with your client, with the attitude that they may or may not fit, but if they do, they may enable the process to take a leap forward.

Sometimes you may even become aware of felt senses in your body that are not yours. This typically happens when your client is not in touch with something he is feeling. In such cases, you can invite your client to notice the feeling in himself, and when he does, you will almost always feel it release in your own body.

Client: She left me a month ago, and I really don't feel much.

Therapist: I don't know if this fits for you, but I'm feeling a heaviness in my chest.

Client: Yes, there is sort of a heaviness. . . . Oh! I had no idea how much anger was there!

Recognizing and acknowledging your own issues. Listening to your client is bound to bring up your own issues. Focusing can help you to recognize and acknowledge your own feelings and reactions as they are triggered by your client's work. In most cases, you will then set these reactions aside and save them for a time when you can do your own processing. There will also be some times, however, when your relationship with your client and his work will be enhanced if you share your personal reactions. In either situation, it can be very important to first be aware of what you are feeling.

There was a time in my early forties when I was in a very emotional process of deciding whether to have a child. One day I was facilitating the Focusing session of a woman who was working on her relationship with her fourteen-year-old son. Suddenly tears welled up in me. Gently and silently I acknowledged my feelings. In just a moment, I was able to give my full attention to the Focuser again. Later, in a Focusing session of my own, I explored the meaning of those feelings and realized they were about my grief that I might never have such a relationship.

Facilitating your presence. The ideal therapeutic relationship depends on your being present as a human being. Your own style and modality will determine how much of your presence you express to your client, and how. But your experience of presence, of being here as a person, will enhance any mode of therapy you use. Being aware in your body brings you into the present moment, into your real, living self—and this is a gift.

Your clients can grow only as much as you do. Use Focusing for yourself, both in your sessions with clients and on your own, and you will enjoy the rewards of being a better therapist and a growing person at the same time.

Chapter Eleven

If You're in Therapy

Now that you know Focusing, you know how to appreciate and honor those moments in your inner work when you feel *something*, even when you don't yet know what it is. You know to not skip those moments, to not be in a hurry to get to something clearer. These are your places of richness, and finding them is like hitting a vein of gold. Psychotherapy is an ideal place to get support as you explore these "fuzzy places" with Focusing.

Many people have found that their therapy is more satisfying after they've learned Focusing. This is true whether or not your therapist has ever heard of Focusing, and whether or not you ever mention Focusing in your sessions. If you're in psychotherapy now, or if you're thinking of starting, here are some ways that Focusing can help your therapy.

How to train your therapist

Some of the processes of Focusing may be different from your therapist's usual way of working. Now that you know Focusing, you can tell your therapist you'd like his or her support in trying something new. You might, for example, want to show him or her this book, and explain that you would like to try this Focusing process in your work. Or you might want to bring in parts of the Focusing attitude, without even mentioning Focusing. Here are some specific things you can ask for.

Starting the session

How do you start your session now? Do you speak first, or does your therapist? Do you talk about what you're feeling right now, or about what has happened since your last session, or about something your therapist brings up?

You might want to tell your therapist you would like to start at least some of your sessions by closing your eyes and quietly sensing in your body. You might say to your therapist that you don't need him or her to say anything during this time. You might invite your therapist to ask you, at the beginning of a session, if you would like to start this way. You might even ask your therapist to guide you through the "attunement" described in Chapter Ten.

One woman reported: "I really like what happens when I remember to feel in my body as I start the session. But often I forget to do that. I get into telling stories about how my week went. So I asked my therapist if she would remind me, by asking 'Do you want to start by sensing your body today?' I feel I'm using the session much more productively when I start it from inside."

Times of quiet

It takes time to sense your body's reaction to something, or to allow a felt sense to form, or to find the right words to describe a feeling. Your therapy sessions need to have pauses in them, times of quiet, so that you can do this inner sensing.

You can tell your therapist there might be times in a session when you are feeling something that takes a little time to put into words, and say that at those times you would like him or her to support you by being quiet with you.

Put bluntly, you are asking your therapist to be willing to shut up sometimes! If your therapist isn't willing to do this, ever, listen carefully to his or her reasons. They might make sense. But if they don't make sense to you, remember you are the person ultimately responsible for your own growth. You have a right to ask for what you need, and to either get it or understand why not.

When you're confused or unclear

Feeling confused or unclear is a signal to sense in your body. Now that you know Focusing, you realize that places of confusion are places of great potential. When you hit something fuzzy inside, something hard to say or hard to describe, that's the place to stay for a while.

However, this is easy to forget; when you're confused, what you're mainly aware of is confusion! You can enlist your therapist's help to remember. You can say to your therapist, "Whenever I'm feeling confused or unclear, I'd like to remember to sense in my body then. It would be great if you would remind me that I can slow down and just stay with the confusion."

Feeling free to say "No, that's not quite right."

Probably you've already noticed that your therapist isn't there to give you answers. She or he is there to give you a safe and supportive place to do your own inner searching. But it can be very easy to slip into an attitude of seeing the therapist as the expert who knows more than you do about the way you should be. This is because our society supports an "expert" model instead of a "partnership" model in most relationships, and it takes courage and consciousness to remember that you are responsible for your own life, no matter what.

The easiest way to remember this, in your therapy, is to check your therapist's words with the feeling in your body and then feel free to say, "No, that's not it," or "That's not quite right, it's more . . ."

You: I don't know why I'm so depressed this week.

Therapist: I wonder if it might have to do with feelings of grief about your separation from your husband.

You: (checking in your body) No, that's not quite it. It is about the separation, but it's not so much grief . . . It's more fear . . . Fear that I'll lose myself again, like I did in that relationship.

Continuing your work between sessions

One of the drawbacks of therapy is that it happens (usually) only one hour a week, and between sessions you have to live your life! Focusing helps you to give your feelings gentle companionship whenever they come up and enables you to do "homework" by continuing your inner work in the times between your therapy sessions.

You may find that strong feelings, like panic or grief, tend to come up late at night, or in the middle of interactions with other people—inconvenient times for calling your therapist. When this happens, just say hello to the feelings. Acknowledge that there must be a good reason for these feelings to come so strongly now. Imagine that you can put a friendly arm around the feelings inside you. Say to yourself, "Yes, part of me feels this way." If you are alone, take time to simply be with the feelings, describing how they feel in your body, and asking, "What do you need me to know right now?" Overwhelming feelings will quickly become manageable with this kind of gentle attention.

If you are with other people when strong feelings come up, first take a deep breath. How often we forget to breathe! Then silently say to the feelings, "Hello, I know you're there." You'll probably find that the feelings relax a little. Depending on your relationship with the people you're with, you may be able to tell them what is happening: "I just got panicky, and I need a little time to breathe." If necessary, you can make an inner appointment with your feelings: "I can't spend time with you right now, but in half an hour I'll be alone in the car and I can listen to you then." Then keep your appointment!

The healing continues

As your therapy progresses, Focusing can support and encourage the positive changes you experience. You will probably find yourself changing and growing in the following ways:

- You are aware of what you are feeling at the time you feel it, rather than feeling numb at the time and having a delayed reaction days or weeks later.

- You feel more accepting of your own opinions and your own perspective, rather than thinking you ought to see the world the way others see it.

- You are more able to have mixed feelings, such as having both fear and excitement about taking the next steps in your life.

- You feel more deserving of love, appreciation, and respect, and you are more able to give these to yourself.

- You have an inner reserve of strength and flexibility, so you are able to handle the ups and downs of life without being crushed.

- You are able to feel happy for long stretches of time without wondering when disaster will strike.

At first, you will probably experience these and other positive changes in small amounts, for short periods of time. Life change often follows the pattern of "two steps forward, one step back." During the times of backsliding, it is easy to doubt whether you are really changing. You can use Focusing to confirm and deepen the experience of positive change. When you notice that you are feeling good, or experiencing some situation in a new way, take time to feel that in your body. Savor the new feeling, name it and welcome it. See also Chapter Six, "Receiving the Gifts," for more about how to deepen your positive experiences.

Be sure to use Focusing to be kind and gentle to yourself during the times when you lose your sense of progress and you're back in the old feelings again. Sometimes the behaviors and attitudes you are releasing will come back strongly just before they let you go—a "last hurrah." Hang in there; you are on your way through!

Becoming your own therapist

Eventually you will be ready to end your therapy. You can use Focusing to help you feel the rightness of this step. Your Focusing skills can help you move from having the support of your therapist to being your own primary support person. Being able to acknowledge your feelings and hear their messages is a lifelong gift, an ability that will stay with you through all the future changes of your life.

Remember, no matter what happens, notice how it feels in your body, and say hello to it. With Focusing, you have a nurturing relationship with your inner self that nothing can take away from you. Enjoy!

Resources

Focusing Networks

These resources can help you connect with other people using Focusing in your area and learn of Focusing workshops and retreats and certification as a Focusing Trainer.

Ann Weiser Cornell, Focusing Resources, 2625 Alcatraz Ave. #202, Berkeley, CA 94705-2702. 510-654-4819. Fax: 510-654-1856.

The Focusing Institute, 220 S. State St. #706, Chicago, IL 60604. 312-986-9700. Fax: 312-986-9701.

The Institute for Bio-Spiritual Research. P. O. Box 741137, Arvada, CO 80006-1137. Tel/Fax: 303-427-5311

Books about Focusing

John Amodeo and Kris Wentworth. *Being Intimate: A Guide to Successful Relationships*. London: Arkana, 1986.
> This book tells how to use Focusing to stay centered and present to yourself in your intimate relationships.

Peter A. Campbell and Edwin M. McMahon. *Bio-Spirituality: Focusing as a Way to Grow*. Chicago: Loyola University Press, 1985.

By two Catholic priests, this is a view of Focusing from a spiritual perspective, in which words like "grace" and "prayer" take on a special meaning.

Ann Weiser Cornell. *The Focusing Guide's Manual*. Third edition. Berkeley, CA: Focusing Resources, 1993. $30 postpaid from Focusing Resources, 2625 Alcatraz Ave. #202, Berkeley, CA 94705-2702. MC/Visa accepted. 510-654-4819.
A manual for guiding people in Focusing with many helpful tips, examples, and charming illustrations.

Neil Friedman. *On Focusing*. 1995. Available from Neil Friedman, 259 Massachusetts Ave., Arlington, MA 02174, for $25 plus $3 shipping and handling in the US.
An excellent resource for both the beginner and the professional.

Eugene Gendlin. *Focusing*. New York: Bantam, 1981.
The original book about Focusing by the man who originated it, well worth reading for many reasons, including its transformative stories about people using Focusing.

Eugene Gendlin. *Let Your Body Interpret Your Dreams*. Wilmette, IL: Chiron Publications, 1986. Available from Chiron Publications, Order Fulfillment, P. O. Box 599, Peru, IL 61354, for $9.95 plus $1.75 shipping and handling.
"Every dream has a gift," says Gendlin, and in this book he teaches how to use Focusing to find the gifts in your dreams, even in the scary ones.

Edwin M. McMahon. *Beyond the Myth of Dominance: An Alternative to a Violent Society*. Kansas City: Sheed and Ward, 1993. (To order: 800-333-7373)
Further writings on "Bio-Spirituality," including the global implications of listening to the felt sense in our lives.

Publications about Focusing

The Focusing Folio. Journal, (with membership), $75 per year from the Focusing Institute, 220 S. State St. #706, Chicago, IL 60604. Edited by Bala Jaison and Mary Lawlor.

The Focusing Connection. Newsletter, $18 per year ($22 overseas), 6 issues, from Focusing Resources, 2625 Alcatraz Ave. #202, Berkeley, CA 94705-2702. Edited by Ann Weiser Cornell. MC/Visa accepted. 510-654-4819.

For Professionals

Eugene Gendlin. *Focusing-Oriented Psychotherapy: A Manual of the Experiential Method.* New York: Guilford, 1996.

Marion N. Hendricks. "Experiencing Level as a Therapeutic Variable." In *Person-Centered Review*, Vol. 1, No. 2, May 1986, 141-162.

Elfie Hinterkopt. *Integrating Spirituality in Counseling: Using the Experiential Focusing Method.* Available from Elfie Hinterkopf, 8200 Neely Dr., #151, Austin, TX 78759. $18 postpaid in the U.S., $21 outside the U.S.

James R. Iberg. "Focusing." In Corsini, R. (ed.), *Handbook of Innovative Psychotherapy.* New York: Wiley, 1981.

Some Other
New Harbinger Titles

Surviving Your Borderline Parent, Item 3287 $14.95

When Anger Hurts, second edition, Item 3449 $16.95

Calming Your Anxious Mind, Item 3384 $12.95

Ending the Depression Cycle, Item 3333 $17.95

Your Surviving Spirit, Item 3570 $18.95

Coping with Anxiety, Item 3201 $10.95

The Agoraphobia Workbook, Item 3236 $19.95

Loving the Self-Absorbed, Item 3546 $14.95

Transforming Anger, Item 352X $10.95

Don't Let Your Emotions Run Your Life, Item 3090 $17.95

Why Can't I Ever Be Good Enough, Item 3147 $13.95

Your Depression Map, Item 3007 $19.95

Successful Problem Solving, Item 3023 $17.95

Working with the Self-Absorbed, Item 2922 $14.95

The Procrastination Workbook, Item 2957 $17.95

Coping with Uncertainty, Item 2965 $11.95

The BDD Workbook, Item 2930 $18.95

You, Your Relationship, and Your ADD, Item 299X $17.95

The Stop Walking on Eggshells Workbook, Item 2760 $18.95

Conquer Your Critical Inner Voice, Item 2876 $15.95

The PTSD Workbook, Item 2825 $17.95

Hypnotize Yourself Out of Pain Now!, Item 2809 $14.95

The Depression Workbook, 2nd edition, Item 268X $19.95

Beating the Senior Blues, Item 2728 $17.95

Call **toll free, 1-800-748-6273,** or log on to our online bookstore at **www.newharbinger.com** to order. Have your Visa or Mastercard number ready. Or send a check for the titles you want to New Harbinger Publications, Inc., 5674 Shattuck Ave., Oakland, CA 94609. Include $4.50 for the first book and 75¢ for each additional book, to cover shipping and handling. (California residents please include appropriate sales tax.) Allow two to five weeks for delivery.

Prices subject to change without notice.